SPELLBOUND

by Robert Morgan Styler

**This book is not
authorized, endorsed, or
sanctioned (and possibly
not even appreciated) by
Equinox International,
Advanced Marketing
Seminars, or
Bill Gouldd.**

Published by
Sandy Creek Publishing

2737 Vista Del Rio
Fallbrook, Ca 92028

Cover and interior design by:
Rob Styler and Bob Knight at Image Zone.
You can reach Image Zone at:
909-676-8644 or www.theimagezone.com

All photographs have been used with the expressed
permission of the photographers.

ISBN# 0-9662373-0-7

The unhealed healer wants gratitude from his brothers, but he is not grateful to them. That is because he thinks he is giving something to them and is not receiving something equally desirable in return. His teaching is limited because he is learning so little. His healing lesson is limited by his own ingratitude, which is a lesson in sickness. True learning is constant.

From *A Course in Miracles*

Decisions made today, echo throughout our lives...

Printed on recycled paper with soy based ink.

Acknowledgements

This book began as a catharsis for me and evolved into a family project. My step-dad, Doug, had a major role in editing and content decisions. My mom was a constant inspiration and found some great quotes. They both spent countless hours helping me turn my thoughts and feelings into a book. My brother, Rick, and his wife, Mary, would wait anxiously for new chapters; their excitement encouraged me to keep writing. My sister, Kendra, congratulated me for leaving Equinox and told me I would be a success at whatever I did. Family is wonderful.

My conversations and laughter with Val Michels began the healing process that led to this book. Jean-Luc Annet has become a best friend and business partner. Larry Michel was an invaluable source of information and ideas. Many people have confirmed stories and offered encouragement, including Jim and Janette Loretto, Joe and JaDee Locke, Sheri Sharman, Paul Channette, Greg Rex, Kale Flagg, Dale Koehrsen, John Alden, Gregg Amerman, Tina Hegadorn, Ally Beasley, and others.

Most of all I would like to thank my son, Kelby, who always reminds me what is important in life.

Rob & Kelby rafting in Mexico.

This book is dedicated to the future of network marketing.

The November 1996 issue of *Inc.* magazine ranked Equinox as the fastest growing privately held company in America. It stated, "Granted it might be easy to write off Bill Gouldd as a smooth-talking con artist. . . . But you'd be foolish to dismiss multilevel marketing out of hand."

Network marketing works, and though my experience with Equinox did not fulfill my dreams, it did expand them. I fell in love with the freedom, income, and personal growth offered by the industry.

I learned a good lesson from the father of one of Equinox's former top producers, Kale Flagg. When Kale first considered network marketing, he sought advice:

"Dad, I'm looking at one of those networking marketing deals."

"You can make a lot of money in those deals, Kale."

"Yeah, but I remember what you always taught us: 'If you play with the pigs you're going to get dirty.' "

"Son, if you were never to get involved in an industry because people had abused it in the past, you could not enter politics, law, construction, religion, or any business. You have to find a group of people who are doing it right and set such a strong example that you change the entire industry."

Like any industry where a lot of money can be made, there are people to admire and people to avoid, there are companies to admire and companies to avoid. Many people are taking the advice of Kale's father and changing the future of network marketing.

I had the honor of meeting one of these ambassadors of change. At twenty-six years old, he grabbed the attention of the industry by quietly producing incredible results. He made a six-figure monthly income within his first six months. John Valenty is the polar opposite of the success model

Bill Gouldd teaches. John is disarming, quiet, and considerate. He built his empire of over 500,000 distributors in less than three years, not by placing unrealistic demands on his people, but by starting people slowly on products and creating loyal customers who turned into business builders.

There is no one company (or opportunity) perfect for everybody. Each company, sponsor, and organization has its own personality and energy.

My decision to join one of the many companies I researched after leaving Equinox is not necessarily a negative reflection on the others. It is simply what felt right to me. I believe in a basic philosophy: "Create your vision, and then play with who shows up."

After what I learned during the last seven years, I will never again follow blindly or passively . . . spellbound.

If you are in a group whose consciousness does not reflect your own, and you are unable at this time to effectively alter the group consciousness, it is wise to leave the group, or the group could lead you. It will go where it wants to go, regardless of where you want to go.

If you cannot find a group whose consciousness matches your own, be the source of one. Others of like consciousness will be drawn to you.

Neale Donald Walsch, *Conversations with God*

Introduction

A good friend asked me, "Rob, if you were still making $20,000 a month, do you think you'd have these ethical concerns?" It's a good question. From the beginning there were situations I chose not to see. They were easier to ignore than acknowledge. Money and power are seductive.

If it were just a few scattered people in the company, I could tolerate the hypocrisy, but I feel it emanates from the core. The attitude is more confused than malicious. Goethe said it well: "Two souls dwell, alas! in my breast." That is how I see Bill Gouldd: his light is blinding and his shadow is deep.

At times I love the man. When he's on stage, he creates fire. I envision we're on a holy crusade to save the planet. My life has purpose. I'm part of a cause. The next minute he's rude, contradictory, and abusive. His intensity spreads across both poles, the positive and the negative, the yin and the yang.

As the industry of network marketing evolves, Equinox must adapt or decay. Tens of thousands of people have been willing to carry Equinox's environmental banner, but with the price of monthly qualifications, seminars, travel, and offices, they were required to run a four-minute mile. Most people could not survive the pace.

I don't regret the last seven years. I learned more than at any other time in my life. Bill Gouldd was a mentor who showed me a different angle on the world. It was a wild ride and an incredible education.

Bill Gouldd taught me, "People will work for money, but they will die for recognition and appreciation of who they are." We often teach what we most need to learn.

In 1996 Equinox was the fastest growing privately held corporation in America. In 1997, most of the top-money earners, Bill Gouldd's loyal following, left—disillusioned and unappreciated.

At one of Equinox's big events, actor Dennis Weaver said, "Money is like manure. If you pile it up, it just stinks. But if you spread it around, it can make beautiful things grow." Imagine if Bill Gouldd had spread the millions around. Imagine if he had kept his promises. Imagine if he had believed his own words. We could have grown beautiful things.

Mr. Gouldd always said, "There are two sides to every story, and the truth usually lies somewhere in the middle." He and I see the world from different perspectives. This book is my story, my truth.

> *'Tis an awkward thing to play with souls,*
> *And matter enough to save one's own.*
> Robert Browning

Bill Gouldd

Chapter 1

Some think it's holding on that makes one strong;
sometimes it's letting go.
Sylvia Robinson

After seven years in "the system," I'm leaving. His phone call catches me off guard.

"Hello, may I help you?" I answer.

"Yeah."

"Excuse me?"

"Yeah."

"Oh, Mr. Gouldd." I struggle to keep my voice from shaking.

"What's going on?" He sounds bored.

"I've decided to sell my distributorship."

"I heard. Top three reasons why?"

I have to compress a decision that I've wrestled with for months into three concise, intelligent reasons. It surprises me how much I still hope to impress him.

"Um, well, first I have been working with Advanced Marketing Seminars and Equinox for over seven years, and out of the thousands of people I have recruited, only two make money on a consistent basis. The marketing plan is too hard. I no longer feel good about bringing people into the system when so few can succeed."

"Next."

"Uh, my experience in Mexico has been frustrating. Before I went down there, I suggested that we needed to adjust the marketing plan to better fit the economy. It's not realistic to expect the same standards to work in both the U.S. and Mexico when our economies are so different. Our sales quotas are hard in the U.S. They're next to impossible in Mexico. I have repeatedly asked, even pleaded, to the corporate office to adjust the plan. I was brushed off with, 'We're looking into it.' More than eighteen months have gone by, and they're still looking into it. Several times I was told, 'We would not be the fastest growing company in the U.S. if we did not know what we were doing.'

"The point is," I continue, "Mexico is not the U.S. We've been down there for almost two years and our sales are embarrassing. I became disillusioned with the attitude of corporate."

"Some things there need to be changed," Mr. Gouldd responds. "Next."

"I've been a paid trainer with Advanced Marketing Seminars for five years. Four months ago there was a trainers' meeting in Vegas, and I wasn't invited. I wasn't even called. I know my checks have gone down since I have been in Mexico, but I was asked to go to down there to help the company. We all knew opening up a new country was going to be difficult. I speak Spanish. I felt an obligation. It's been hard, but I have a seven-year track record with this company. I don't want to be evaluated solely by the amount of my last check."

"I would put your third reason first," he notes. "You're feeling hurt and unappreciated. I don't know why you weren't invited. I'll call Steve and ask. It's nothing personal. Don't be so damn sensitive. It was nothing you haven't heard twenty times before at other trainers' meetings. It was no big deal, Rob."

"I don't feel good about what I am doing," I continue, trying to make him understand. "I cannot look someone in the eye and tell them the best decision they could possibly make is to follow the system. I've seen too many people in the system get hurt."

"People get hurt everywhere, Rob," he replies with an annoyed tone. "What are you going to do, go back to the Peace Corps? Is that safe enough for you? We are trying to change people's lives, to make a difference, to make an impact on this planet. Would you rather sell cars where nobody really gets hurt but you make no real difference in anybody's life, where you have no long-term impact? People fail in everything. We give them a road map to success. If they don't follow it correctly or long enough, why should you feel guilty?"

"I just don't believe in the system anymore. There is too much manipulation through fear and intimidation. I've been verbally and mentally abused too many times. You always ask for ideas on the executive conference calls, but whenever someone comes up with an idea, you call them a fucking idiot."

"Just because you always came up with fucking stupid ideas, Rob, don't blame my system."

I don't know how to respond to this—it's too ironic. Expecting him to go on, I don't say anything. After what feels like a minute, I continue.

"After seven years and thousands of people in my sales force, I have only two who make money consistently. Obviously, I have to take some responsibility, but my story is similar to others."

"Who are your two people making money?"

"Seana and Dr. Cohn—I mean Howie. And Seana makes most of her money because of Howie."

"And why does Howie do so well?"

"Because he's talented."

"Fuck you, Rob. The only reason Howie makes money is because I spend personal time with him. I spend about one day with him every two months, and he kicks most of your asses every month, and he only works part time. That to me is scary. This system works for one reason: me. When I am focused and active the whole company gets on track. When I take some time off, which I deserve, everything goes to shit."

"Well, that is also one of the reasons I'm leaving," I respond. "The system and the company depend completely on you. It's not duplicable."

"It does not just depend on me!"

"You just said it did!"

"The system works. Period. All I need are the right people to follow it correctly. I just got a video of Rich Von doing a briefing and that little fucker did not even mention my name until the last part. That little piece of shit was drilling holes when he met me and now he doesn't even fucking mention my name." [As I write this book, Rich Von is a multimillionaire, and his organization was responsible for about 50 percent of Equinox's total sales last year. Obviously unappreciated, he left Equinox four months after I did to

11

start a new company: Trek Alliance.] "All I need is one fucking person with the vision and the balls to follow my system and not forget where they came from when they reach success. One fucking person."

"Well, the one thing you have always taught us, Mr. Gouldd, is that the only thing that counts is results. If you've been teaching the same system now for sixteen years, and not one person has followed it correctly, maybe it is not the people. Maybe there is something wrong with the system." Oh, damn, that feels good! For the first time, I push his buttons, instead of him pushing mine.

"Fuck you, Rob. The system works. I'll tell you one person who's doing this thing right: Buck Reed. That man has a bright future with this company. I only need to tell that man something once and he does it. No questions asked. All you other fuckers have your opinions and ideas. I have to tell you the same fucking thing ten times and you still don't learn. We are the fucking fastest growing company in America. We have broken all of the records. Who else do you know personally who is worth three hundred million dollars? Who, Rob? Who?"

"You are the only one, sir."

"That's fucking right that I'm the only one." He pauses. "You know, it amazes me how stupid you are. You've been away from the battery for over a year, busting your tail in Mexico with no tangible results. You're burnt out. Everybody's been sucking your energy. Rather than coming back to the States, getting back in the system, and saying, 'I'm beat; pump me back up; tag-team, and send someone else down there.' You just want to quit. Give up. Throw everything away. Everything you have built over the last seven years—gone!—because you don't feel good."

"I cannot sell the system anymore." I try again to make him understand. "I don't believe in it. I just want to sell my organization, be compensated for what I've built, and do other things with my life."

"You never gave me the five years I asked for. You would get to work, start building momentum, your checks would get up, and then you would meet some girl and get off track. You couldn't keep your dick in your pants, and you would fuck your business away."

"That's not true, and you know it." I want to say that I'm not the one with that problem. I restrain myself. I don't want to touch the women issue. He doesn't either. He changes the subject.

"Okay. So you want to quit. You want to sell your organization. You're not going to get a million dollars for it."

"I don't expect to get a million dollars for it."

"Do you have a buyer?"

"I talked to Seth and Sheri. They're both interested, and Seana also wants to buy it."

"Sell it. I think you should. You've never been a great producer. You're not our worst, but you've never been great. Mediocre would be the best word." He knows this always used to motivate me. But this time, I'm detached. I don't react. I almost feel I'm in control.

"If I was mediocre, why did you hand-select me and pay me to train thousands of people in your company for five years?"

"Rob, you never reached your potential. Now you are going to run away. What do you think you're going to do?"

"I don't know. I just know I am not happy with what I am doing. So I want to change."

"You're out in the middle of the fucking ocean, and you want to jump out of the ship you're on—with no sight of land? This is the type of shit that keeps me up at night. You've worked with me for seven years, and you are so fucking stupid that you want to cut your balls off before you know where you are going to stick your dick." Only Bill Gouldd would use that analogy. And, as I'm sure he planned, it makes me react.

"I have a plan."

"What?"

"It is not something I want to discuss with you right now."

"Ha. Bye, Rob." He hangs up the phone.

Money does not change the sickness, only the symptoms.
John Steinbeck

Chapter 2

That I feed the hungry, forgive an insult, and love my enemy—
these are great virtues.
But what if I should discover that the poorest of beggars and most
impudent offenders
are all within me, and that I stand in need of the alms of my own
kindness;
that I myself am the enemy who must be loved—
what then?

Carl Jung

My story begins in Guatemala. Marina and I meet in a small village where I am stationed with the Peace Corps. She is educated, innocent, and beautiful; I am lonely. Eight months after we meet, we marry.

After purchasing fifty acres in a valley of Guatemala, we go home to San Diego, planning to earn some money in the States and return to a simple life of farming. Money's not important. I want to live lightly on the land, sing "Kumbaya," and be happy.

Instead, I meet Bill Gouldd.

Marina has some medical complications that require two surgeries. We have no health insurance and quickly find ourselves $25,000 in debt. One of her conditions is complicated by endometriosis, a condition aggravated every month with menses. The monthly pain increases until the doctor suggests pregnancy as a cure. With about as much thought as we had put into getting married, we decide to become parents. One month later we're pregnant.

We're excited. My parents are excited. Her parents are excited. But the day we go back to the doctor is sobering.

"Your wife needs prenatal care. Her pregnancy may be complicated because of the endometriosis, but you have no health insurance, and we don't believe you can pay." He waits for a response. None comes.

"What I'm saying is, *I will not treat her*. I did get some forms you can fill out to get aid from the state."

I am sitting in the left chair, Marina the right. We face the doctor who sits behind his large metal desk. I can tell he wants us to leave. I want to leave, but my muscles don't respond. All I can see is the little vein on his temple pulsating up and down. It doesn't seem real. I feel helpless and small. The details of his office etch in my memory. I leave in a daze and walk toward the only sanctuary I can think of, a place to be alone, the bathroom.

I close the lid, sit down on the toilet, and cry. I think back over the twenty-five years of my life. I feel like a complete failure. I'm living with my parents because I have no money for rent. I'm driving a car I had to name so I can yell encouragement on long uphill drives. I'm $25,000 in debt, and I'm earning less than $8 an hour. My wife needs medical care I cannot afford, and I am already failing to provide for my unborn child.

This is not supposed to happen. I was an Academic All-American. I have international experience in the Peace Corps. I'm bilingual. My dad was a doctor. My step-dad is a professor. I'm supposed to be a success.

I feel sorry for myself for about ten minutes, go over to the mirror, look at my tear-streaked face and think, *Never again. Never again is someone going to treat me that way because I don't have money. Never.*

The next morning I open the classified section of the paper to find my fortune. Most of the ads show little promise, but there are a few that intrigue me. The first one reads as follows:

SPORTSMINDED
Intl. environmental firm looking for
dynamic people who want a change.
Unlimited income.

I am an athlete. I love the environment. Unlimited income. Bingo!

I call. "You have reached our marketing department. Due to the extremely high volume of calls, you are being routed to our automatic voice mail. Please leave your name, message, and the best time to call you back."

The voice is deep and relaxed. It sounds confident. The company must be growing like crazy if nobody has time to answer the phone. I leave an enthusiastic message asking them to please call me back.

DRIVE A MERCEDES
Looking for motivated people who want to make $100,000 (or more) a year.

This one seems out of my league, but I call anyway. "Due to the extremely high volume of calls, you have been routed to our automatic voice mail. Please leave a message, and your call will be returned in the order it was received."

Well, they obviously need more people to handle these calls. Maybe I'll get lucky. I leave another message.

$250,000/yr
I used to be a pre-school teacher and this is what I made my first year with this incredible company. I'm looking for others who want to do the same.

I'm amazed that there are this many opportunities to make big money. Why am I working as a bilingual instructional aide making $7.47 an hour? I call. "You have reached our marketing department . . . " I start to see a pattern. They're all similar, overly perky messages. They all have enticing, vague ads. Most of the phone numbers are similar. These ads are all from the same company.

I leave another enthusiastic message. Monday, nobody calls me back. Tuesday and Wednesday, nobody calls me back. Every day, I'm leaving new messages asking them to please call me back. Finally, Thursday at 6 P.M., the phone rings.

"Hi, this is Dawn Smith. I am calling for Rob Styler."

"That's me. Are you the one from the company?"

"Well, yeah, you called about our advertisement."

"Great, how do I get there and when is the soonest I can come for an interview?"

"Seven-thirty tonight." She sounds confused.

"You're kidding. Tonight! YES! I knew this was going to be a great day."

It doesn't enter my mind that most companies do not interview at 7:30 on Thursday night. I get directions, put on my best Peace Corps T-shirt, and jump in "Pegasus." Pegasus is my '82 Toyota Tercel. I have to keep the window open and put my arm on the outside of the door to keep it from shaking loose. With wind roaring through the car, it always makes me hum the song from *The Wizard of Oz* when the flying monkeys are after Dorothy. "Dun-da-dun-da-daa-dun, Dun-da-dun-da-daa-dun, Dun-da-dun-da-da-dun-dun."

I arrive with my long hair, my beard, and my Birkenstocks, ready for my first job interview. The parking lot is full and the building is large, impressive, with lots of glass. My enthusiasm is overtaken by doubt. *What am I doing here? I've no experience. Who am I kidding?*

I go up to the second floor and knock on the door. Nobody answers. I can hear a lot of activity inside. I peek in and a gorgeous woman sitting behind the desk looks at me sweetly, as if to say it's okay, come on in, we won't hurt you.

"I . . . I . . . I have an interview." Ever since I was little I've stuttered, usually at the most inopportune moments.

"Come on in. Just sign in here. Who is your interview with?" There are so many people milling around. Everybody seems happy and excited. It feels more like a cocktail party than a business.

"Who is your interview with?"

"Oh, excuse me. Dawn, Dawn Smith."

"Oh, she's a wonderful lady. You'll really like her. Just take a seat on the couch, she'll be here in a minute." The couch is full, so I lean against the wall. Actually, I slide behind the plant. Looking at all of the suits and ties, I suddenly wish I had worn my running shoes instead of my Birkenstocks.

"Hi, I'm Dawn! You sounded so great on the phone. I've really been looking forward to meeting you." I hardly said three words on the phone, but I'm glad she's friendly. She shows me around the office and introduces me to the "associates." I begin to forget my attire and am amazed at how friendly everyone is—almost too friendly.

When I came back from Guatemala, I experienced culture shock in the shampoo aisle at the supermarket: I stared, completely disoriented by the number of choices. Now I am just as confused as each person compliments me, then compliments each other, then praises the company. I've found HappyLand.

I don't know what they do, but I know I want to be part of it.

When I grow up, I want to be a little boy.
William James

Chapter 3

The Soul selects her own Society—
Then—shuts the Door—
To her divine Majority—
Present no more. . . .

Emily Dickinson

There are about sixty people milling around what looks like a lunchroom. Dawn runs off to do something, and I am left on my own to explore. There's a large, oval, wood plaque that's hand-painted with dolphins and whales. The print at the bottom reads, WE DO NOT INHERIT THE EARTH FROM OUR PARENTS. WE ARE BORROWING IT FROM OUR CHILDREN. I like this place.

Someone announces that the briefing is about to start. Everyone starts migrating toward two large double doors. I hear someone whisper to my right, "Let's hurry. I want to make sure you get a seat." I don't know what's going on, but I know I'm going to get a seat. Maybe this is part of the interview, a creative way to test our assertiveness. I take two long steps to the left, hop over the coffee table, make a quick sideways move to the right, and I'm in: second row, third chair from the right.

There are about 100 chairs and 120 people. I think twenty people have just been eliminated from the competition. They've failed the musical chairs part of the interview.

"Hi, I'm Casey. Is this your first time?" An attractive blond with way too much energy is bouncing in the chair to my right.

"First time for what?" I respond.

"First time to hear the briefing. I remember my first time. I didn't think I could do it. I was so intimidated. I used to be a hairdresser for Vidal Sassoon." She leans closer and says in a lower voice, "I had purple hair the first time I came in. Really I did. Twelve earrings up my ear. But Sheri made me feel special. This company has changed my life. You're going to love it."

Confused, I look at her. I'm sure she's telling me about her purple hair to make me feel better about my Birkenstocks and T-shirt.

"What is this company that I'm going to love?" I finally respond.

"It's funny you ask that. I'm still not sure. I'm not even sure what I'm doing or how I get paid. All I know is I made more money last month than I ever did as a hairdresser."

Now I'm curious. What is this place, and who is Sheri?

Half of the people start clapping, and then the rest of us start clapping. I don't know why I'm clapping. I'm just clapping.

A well-dressed, jovial man steps to the front of the room, "I'm sure most of you are more accustomed to a one-on-one interview. At the pace we're growing, as you can see, that would be impossible. My name is James Hilgensen, and I am going to explain, to the best of my ability, this incredible opportunity."

Casey is laughing at every little joke, raising her hand high at every rhetorical question, and looking intently at the speaker.

"How many of you drink water?" My hand is up and high. I figure Casey already got the job; I'll just follow her lead.

"How many of you bathe?" More hands raise, and laughter ripples through the crowd.

"If the person next to you didn't raise their hand, you can move." More laughter.

He puts in a video with Rex Allen, Sr. His voice is familiar from nature shows. Rex explains, "Water is our friend. We just haven't treated our old friend very well. That is why we need our new friends at National Safety Associates." The video is simplistic, warm, and hokey.

James pops out the video. "I know some of you might be thinking, *Water filters. I don't want to sell water filters.* When I first sat where you're sitting, that was the first thing I thought, but I listened and learned. In the United States, four billion dollars—that's billion with a B—was spent last year on bottled water. That's more money than all of the ticket sales for all of the movie theaters nationwide combined."

Wow.

"The four biggest players in the bottled water industry are Coca-Cola, Pepsi Cola, Beatrice Foods, and Anheuser Busch. Do you think they're in it for our health or the money?"

"The money," I find myself saying with the crowd.

"That's right, the money. How many of you could use some more money?" I am reaching for the ceiling.

If I could show you a way to make an extra thousand dollars this weekend, would you be interested?" I'm ready to jump over the first row and hug the man.

"It's simple, and I'll show you how. We are here to train you. Wealth is not only for the privileged, but for the informed and inspired."

I'm inspired. I just want to be informed.

"It's simple, but simplicity is power. How many of you like to give your opinion, even when no one asks for it?" More scattered laughter. It seems like the laughter is always coming from the same people. Casey is by far the most enthusiastic, almost like the company cheerleader.

"All we do is give people this filter to try free for three days and ask for their opinion. It's that simple. When we hook it up, we do a quick demonstration. We take some water from the tap. We take some water from the filter. And then we do a pool chlorine test." As he's speaking, he pours water from two jars into two glasses. "This just shows the level of chlorine. How many of you have a pool or Jacuzzi?" A few hands go up. "How many of you would like to have a pool or Jacuzzi?" Almost every hand is raised with laughter.

He puts ten drops in each glass; the tap water turns yellow while the filtered water stays crystal clear. *Wow.* The crowd reacts, mostly the same people who are always laughing, with "oohs," "aahs," and "can you believe that?"

"If you had a choice, which one would you drink?" He holds up the two glasses. One is a bright yellow color now, the other still crystal clear. "We have a saying: 'Either buy a filter, or be a filter.' If you or your loved ones do not have a filter, these chemicals are going in your body every day, day after day after day. We don't do something today and get sick tomorrow. We do something over and over for fifteen years. Suddenly the doctor tells us we have cancer, or a heart condition, or some other life-threatening, life-altering disease, and we think, *Where did that come from?* Our job is to educate people about problems in the environment and offer simple, cost-effective solutions. Oh, by the way, we can also make fortunes doing it."

I *have* found HappyLand. I get to solve environmental problems, help people, and make a fortune! I loved the Peace Corps, but it paid me only $200 a month.

Now he starts to explain what he calls "the marketing plan." Again, I begin to wonder if I'm qualified. There are a lot of numbers and percentages. I never liked math.

Casey leans closer and whispers, "I still don't understand this stuff, but they keep sending me checks." I feel better.

After the marketing plan, James draws six circles down the right side of the whiteboard and explains how most companies suffer from a phenomenon called "whisper down the lane." This is where one person whispers to another person who whispers to another, and the story changes along the way.

"Scientists tell us that humans can retain only seven to ten percent of what they hear on a first-time basis. Let's be generous and call it fifty percent. If Joe, who is a doctor, knows one hundred percent of the information, and he teaches Suzy who is a nurse, she now retains fifty percent of the information. Remember we're being generous. Now she teaches John, her plumber. John retains twenty-five percent of the original information, but how much does John think he knows? That's right, one hundred percent—and that's the problem. But wait, it gets worse. John then talks to one of his buddies who now retains twelve percent. For the next person it's six percent. And then, our well-meaning next door neighbor sells us on a business opportunity of which he understands only three percent of the correct, original information. We naively follow him and unfortunately fail. Not because the business wasn't good but because the training wasn't good." *So I just need the right training.*

"If you want to be a doctor, but your next door neighbor who is a plumber offers you a discount on training, can you really blame the medical profession if you kill your first three patients?"

"No," responds the crowd.

"Success is the simplest thing in the world. You just have to find someone who has what you want, and do what they do. If you have not experienced the success you want in your life, it is because you're learning from the wrong people. Did you know that if you graduate from college in the United States of America, you decrease your chance of becoming a millionaire by eighty percent?" *Wow.* "How many of us wish we'd known that before we went to college?!"

"Yeah!"

I'm with him now. I went to college. I graduated with highest honors and I'm broke. But it's not my fault. I've just been learning from the wrong people. Now I can learn from the right people in HappyLand.

"We solve that problem. We learn directly from the source. One hundred percent of the information comes from the master of this industry, Bill Gouldd." James draws a star to the left of the circles with arrows going from the star directly to all of the circles.

"This gives you two major advantages. First, it doesn't matter who invited you down here because you are going to learn directly from the source. Second, you can find people better than you—all you have to do is get them to an Advanced Marketing seminar, and Bill Gouldd will train them personally for you. How many of you would like to have people who are part of your company, people who are going to make you money, personally trained by a self-made multimillionaire?"

"Yes!" I respond with the crowd.

I'm excited. Not only am I going to be trained by the right person, but he will train the people I recruit, too. I look excitedly over to Casey.

She whispers, "This is the best part. I just drag in bodies and make money. They call me the body dragger. I have fun and make money. I still don't know what I am doing." This is the third time she has said that. I'm beginning to believe her.

"Could we have a few people come up to the front and share your personal story of what's happened to you since you joined the company? Come on, don't be shy."

Casey gets up and so do a few others. Casey is the first to speak.

"I was a hairdresser for Vidal Sassoon for years. Because of all of the chemicals in that industry, I got a lung infection. The doctor told me I had to change careers or die. I've had dyslexia since I was a child, so I don't read or write very well. I was so scared looking through the want ads. I wasn't qualified for anything. I answered an ad that said, 'Crazy,' and believe me, that's me. I met Sheri Sharman and Bill Gouldd, and what has happened is just incredible. I still don't understand how, but last month I made twelve thousand dollars."

I'm in shock. The cheerleader made $12,000. I still don't completely understand what they're doing, but I now know I'm doing it, too.

I barely hear the other testimonials. My mind is still focused on how much $12,000 will change my life. The briefing ends with applause, and Dawn asks me to "join her circle." I've no idea what she means, but I follow. All of the chairs have been rearranged from rows to circles, and in each group of three to fifteen people, one person is drawing circles on his or her notepad and talking excitedly to the others.

Dawn leads me to a group with about eight people. She begins to sell us on this great opportunity. I'm thinking, "Just tell me if I got the job." She keeps selling and then begins to tell us how wonderful Seth Bowen is (her "sponsor"). She's going on and on. Finally, I interrupt.

"Dawn, I don't mean to be rude, but if you could just tell me how to apply, I would like to get started as soon as possible."

"So, you're ready to get started now?"

"If you guys want me. I was ready to get started twenty minutes ago."

"Why don't you go take a seat on the couch, and I'll be with you in just a few minutes."

I'm sitting alone on the couch thinking, *Damn, I said the wrong thing. I was too pushy, and now I blew it. They just didn't want to embarrass me in front of the other applicants.*

Dawn comes over after five minutes. "Come here, I want to introduce you to Sheri." I'm excited and scared. Did I do something good or something bad?

"Sheri, this is Rob. Tonight is his first night, and he's ready to get started right away."

"Great, Rob, it's a pleasure to meet you." This woman emanates warmth and radiance. Her desk is covered with crystals and dolphins. We shake hands, and she continues.

"Isn't this exciting? He's got what it takes, Dawn. You found a winner, your diamond in the rough. I want to work personally with him. Rob, we're going to make you a leader in this company. What do you think about that?"

"Sounds great to me. Just tell me what to do."

"I like you. It's great meeting you, Rob."

I walk away stunned. Like being touched by an angel.

Dawn looks at me with wide eyes. "I can't believe she said that. Sheri never says that. She must see something really special in you. Let's get your paperwork filled out and get you started right away."

We go back to the kitchen area and find a narrow, empty space on a big, fake-marble table. About fifteen other people are filling out their paperwork.

"Just complete your application. It only costs twenty dollars."

"Wait a minute. I have to pay to apply? What if I don't get the job? Do I get my money back?" The people who seem to work with the company react with wide eyes and clenched jaws, looking at Dawn as if they want me separated from the herd.

She continues calmly, "If you fill out the application, you're automatically enrolled."

"You mean anybody who fills out the application gets the job?"

"We're growing so fast, our biggest problem is finding enough quality people. You definitely qualify."

I fill out my application and hand over my $20.

"Now, where do you want to start?"

"Um, here. Or do you have other offices in San Diego? This was a little bit of a drive." I decide not to tell her about Pegasus.

"No, I mean where in the marketing plan do you want to start?"

"What do you mean?"

"Well, you have different options. You can start out as a 'Dealer' and just get a little bit of product or, if you really want to make money, you can start out as a 'Manager'."

"I really want to make money!"

"Okay. To start as a Manager, it's a five-thousand-dollar investment in product inventory. You get a twenty percent rebate back from the company, so it's really only four thousand dollars, and once you reach the position, you never have to re-qualify."

"What?"

"Once you're a Manager you never have to re-qualify."

"I got that part. It's the first part I'm lost on. You want me to give you five thousand dollars?"

"You're not giving it to me. You're investing in your own future. Here, let me have you talk to Casey."

Casey bounces over. "I knew you were going to love this. As soon as I sat down, I could see passion in your eyes. So, you're going to start as a Manager, right?"

"Is the Manager where I have to give somebody five thousand dollars?"

"I know, I thought the same thing: How can I pay more money when I'm already broke?"

"Exactly."

"What they showed me was that the reason I was broke was that I'd

26

never invested in myself before. I had invested in beauty school, in my car, in my clothes, but never in myself. When I invested my five thousand dollars—actually it was my dad's—it was the best thing I've ever done in my life."

"But I don't have five thousand dollars."

"That's okay. Who do you know who does? Remember the part in the briefing: Other people's ideas, other people's efforts, and other people's money. OPI, OPE, and OPM. Those are the three keys to success."

At this point, I don't remember anything about the briefing. All I know is I don't have five thousand dollars.

"Do I have to invest five thousand dollars?" I ask.

"No, not at all. Let me have you talk to Seth Bowen." I feel like I'm at a car dealership being handed off to the next closer.

As soon as Seth speaks, I know he is the voice on the message of the first ad that I called. "Hi. Dawn and Sheri are both very impressed with you. You must be an amazing individual to make such a strong impression so quickly." Again, the compliments. I begin to relax. Seth is tall and well-dressed.

"I understand you want to get started, but five thousand dollars might be a little much for you right now. What would you be comfortable with?"

"I would be comfortable with working for you and getting paid for it."

"Well, I can appreciate that, but that's the beauty of this business. You don't work for me. You work for yourself. And you work with me and Casey, and with Dawn and Sheri, and even Mr. Gouldd. We all work as a team. You'll be working for yourself, but not by yourself. What you're doing is investing in your own business, your own future."

"But I have nothing to invest!"

"I understand. My life used to be filled with *buts*, also. 'I would like to, *but.*' 'I want to buy that, *but.*' 'I would like to take a vacation, *but.*' Bill Gouldd taught me how to start saying *yes*, and it has been amazing what has happened over just the last few months. Now, do you want to say *but* or *yes?*"

"Yes, but I don't have any money."

He laughs. "We're making progress; now you say *yes* and *but* together.

You see, we all have patterns that have kept us from success in the past. I obviously don't know you well, but I would guess that you have a pattern of making excuses that keeps your mind from finding solutions. If you had to find money, where would you look?"

"How much do I need?"

"Whatever you're comfortable with."

"I could probably come up with a few hundred bucks." I've no idea where I can find that kind of money, but at least we're not talking about $5,000 anymore.

"One of the amazing things the company does is they offer you an automatic five-hundred-dollar line of credit."

"They're going to give me five hundred dollars to get started?"

"Well, sort of. It's a line of credit."

"Are they going to check my credit?"

"Not at all."

"I'm in. Just tell me where to sign." Regarding debt, I'm already in a pit with twelve alligators. If I can buy a rope, it's worth risking one more 'gator.

"The way it works is, for every dollar you put in, they match you with a dollar. So if you can only come up with a hundred dollars, the company will then give you a hundred dollars line of credit. Now you'll have two hundred dollars in product to start your business. We call it 'courtesy credit.' It is just one of the ways we help you get your business started. Now, you said you could come up with a few hundred dollars, so I imagine you want to maximize the credit line, right?"

He's got me there. I did say I could come up with a few hundred dollars, and I don't want to look wishy-washy. *Think. Think. Stall.*

"If I give you this money, then I get product that I can sell to make more money." I'm starting to figure this thing out. I have a plan.

"Exactly."

I had overheard a conversation about the product being shipped. "Okay.

I have the money. But for me to give it to you, I have to get the product tonight. I'm not going to give you my money and wait ten days for my product to be shipped. If I can get the product tonight, deal. If not, when you have the product in hand, I'll give you the money."

"Perfect." Seth responds enthusiastically. "I have the product in my car." Damn. Bad plan.

"Okay, but you have to do me a favor. I have to transfer some money, and it won't be in my checking account until Monday. I . . . I . . . I need you to not deposit the check till Monday. You . . . you . . . you can do that, right?" I hate that stuttering.

"Sure."

I've no money in my checking account and definitely no other accounts from which to transfer money, but it buys me some time. I learn my first of many lessons in creative financing. I figure I'll get the product tonight. I'll have to work tomorrow but I'll have all night Friday, and then the whole weekend, to sell the water filters and deposit the money in my account. And I have to sell only three filters to cover the check. When I turn that water yellow, everybody is going to buy one.

I'm wondering if my car is big enough. With all of the filters I'm going to be selling, I might need a bigger car. Well, with all of the money I'm going to make, I can buy a bigger car. This is great. HappyLand.

By the time I fill out my paperwork, sign the contract, and get my product, it's about 11 P.M. I carry my box of filters to the bathroom with me, and as I leave I look in the mirror and think, *This is it. I've found my opportunity. Financial freedom. Now it's up to me to make it happen.*

I get in the elevator and place my box of filters on the handrail. My back is facing the door. The elevator fills with excited people talking about the night's events. I hear Dawn's voice: "I can't believe it. I've been doing this business for two months and nobody has signed up. Then tonight, bang. This guy not only signs up, he buys product the same night. Can you believe that? I can't believe I was thinking about quitting."

The elevator is full; she must not see me. I stare at the wall of doubt in front of me. Her friends motion toward me.

"Oh, Rob." She pauses, obviously surprised. "I'm just so excited about you. You know most people don't know what they want in life, but it's obvious you know how to make a decision. That is one of the most important traits for success."

"Yeah, Rob. You're going to do great."

"Congratulations, Rob. This is the first step to a bright future."

"Best thing you could have done, Rob."

Each person shares his and her reassurances as they leave the elevator, but the first seed of doubt is planted. *Why hadn't anybody else signed up in two months? Am I doing the right thing? What if I can't sell the filters?*

Those who fear to suffer, already suffer from fear.
Montaigne

Chapter 4

Everything is possible if you wish hard enough.
Peter Pan

The fresh air of Pegasus blows away any doubt. I get home at midnight, excited.

"Did you get the job?" Marina asks in Spanish.

"Not only did I get a job, but I got you one, too."

"*Comó?* How am I going to work? I hardly speak English."

"That's okay. There are a lot of people in California who speak Spanish, and they told me they need people who speak Spanish fluently. That's you, *chica.*"

"No, Rob. You do it. I don't want to."

"Come on. It'll be fun. We can work together. Build a future together. We'll have a great time."

"We'll see."

That is always her way of ending the conversation.

The morning brings new doubt.

"How did your interview go last night?" My mom asks from the kitchen.

"Mom, it was amazing. They turned the water yellow. They showed a video about water pollution. We have been drinking poisons. This company is breaking all the records. I sat right next to a lady who made twelve thousand dollars last month. I'm so excited. This is my answer."

"It's great you're excited, but what is this company?"

"It's a company that's saving the planet. I'm going to be my own boss. I work for myself but not by myself. This millionaire Bill Gouldd is going to train me directly so I don't have to deal with whisper down the lane."

"I can tell you're excited, but I still don't understand."

"I don't understand everything, either. I'm going back for training on Saturday. They're going to train me to be a leader. Mom, you would not believe how excited these people were. All I have to do is get five people who get five people who get five people and I can make a fortune."

"It sounds like something one of your cousins did once. Do you have to recruit people and buy stuff, and the more people you recruit, the more money you make?"

"Yeah, exactly."

"I know those things sound exciting, Rob, but they're illegal. A lot of people have been put in jail."

"Mom, this must be something different, because it's a real business. They had their own video. They've been around for twenty years. If they were illegal, I think someone would have figured it out by now."

"Maybe it is not illegal, but it sounds like one of those pyramids. They get you all excited and hyped up, but all they want is your money. You didn't give them any money, did you?"

"Mom, how can I give them something I don't have? You, of all people, know I'm broke." This was true. I gave them a check with no funds, so I technically gave them no money. But I start to wonder. They did seem anxious to have me sign that contract and hand over the check.

"Those kind of companies sublease office space, take all the money they can in one city, and take off before they get caught. You need a real job with a salary, Rob. You're going to be a father soon. You have to start to be more responsible."

The R-word. It keeps creeping into my life. I'm a husband, and soon I'll be a father. I have a sudden urge to grab my backpack, head to Europe, jump on the Eurail, and travel. My escape is prevented because I've sold my backpack, have no money for the flight, and am too old for the Eurail student discount.

I think about the water filters in my trunk. *I'll tell Mom I got a sample one. Once she sees the demo, she'll know it's legit.*

"I'll be right back." I run to the car.

"Mom, you have to see this. You won't even believe it."

"You're right. I probably won't." We both smile.

"This little wonder turns toxic tap water into pure mountain spring water for pennies a gallon. Did you ever think you would pay more for bottled water than you do for gasoline? Many people do, people who haven't met me yet." I said it fast, like a salesman. "I learned all that last night. Pretty good, huh?"

"You're a natural. So I'm supposed to buy one of these."

"Either that or hand me my first failure as I begin my budding business venture. Slap defeat in my face as I take my first tentative step. Throw my seeds of hope upon the hot, dry cement of your indifference. Create a pattern of failure that will almost guarantee that my growing family and I will have to live with you the rest of our lives." I give her the puppy dog look. It always works.

"How much is it?"

"Normally, it's two hundred and twenty dollars, but because you're my mom and all, and my first sale, in commemoration of this historic event, I will sell it to you at my special wholesale cost of one hundred and thirty."

She buys it. My first sale. I run downstairs to my wife. "I made my first sale."

"Great, how much money did you make!"

I didn't think about that. I had sold it at my cost, but I hadn't included shipping or tax, so I'd lost money. I'd actually lost money on my first sale.

I can hardly sleep Friday night. I'm going to get trained by a multimillionaire. Everything is going to work out.

I get up early, trim my beard a little. This time I put on my running shoes and iron my jeans and T-shirt. I'm looking good.

Pegasus is in rare form, and I get there fifteen minutes early. It's 8:45 in the morning, and there's not a car in the parking lot. I go up to the second floor and the San Diego Marketing sign has been taken off the door. Just the old, squiggly line of glue remains where the sign used to be. My mom's warnings about "here today, gone tomorrow" echo in my mind. The door is locked. I lean with my back against the door and slide to the ground. I rock back and forth in the fetal position. *They set this whole thing up just to get my six hundred bucks. It's like* The Sting *and I'm the sucker. Mom's right again. But the joke's on them. That check will bounce.*

I'm not upset about the money. It's my dream I lost.

I curl against the door, thinking. I'm not sure how much time passes. I hear a car park outside. As they come out of the elevator, I recognize the people from the other night. One's name is Joe, the other Marc.

"What's wrong? You look upset."

I stare at both of them.

"It's Rob, right? Here, get off the floor. What's going on?" Joe helps me up.

"Well, when I got here there were no cars, and then the sign was off the door and the door was locked. Training was supposed to start at 9 A.M. I thought you guys skipped town."

"Dude, no way. You just got here way early. Remember in the briefing where he said we only remember seven to ten percent of what we hear? You're living proof. Training starts at ten. You're just an eager beaver. That's cool. Sheri is going to like this guy." Marc again begins with the compliments.

"What about the sign?"

"It got a scratch so we're fixing it. Did somebody feed you with some doubt? Don't worry; it happens. We call 'em 'dream stealers.' Dude, my parents were so neg when I got started. I couldn't even talk to 'em for a while because they were bumming me out."

Joe pats me on the back. "Come on in, you can help us set up. We're not really supposed to let new people in this early, but you're cool."

I help set up the chairs, change water for the demo, and cue the video. Then I smell something. It smells like marijuana.

Marc is walking around the office holding an abalone shell with smoke billowing out of it. He's saying some prayer about white light and making sure the smoke gets in every corner of the room. This is weird.

"Guys, do you think it's a good idea to have that kind of smoke in here before the people come for training?" I've always been phobic about drugs.

Marc responds in a fake Rastafarian accent, "He thinks it's the herb, mon. People always think that the first time. You need to relax and let the smoke clear your energy. Your negative thoughts and emotions will be washed away, mon."

"Don't freak him out, Marc. He's new. I'll explain it to you, Rob."

Joe sets the stage. "When Bill Gouldd and Sheri first started in this office everything clicked. It just worked. When he finished a briefing, everybody signed up. They did over two hundred thousand dollars in volume in the first three weeks. Mr. Gouldd got a check, his first month's check, for over sixty-two thousand dollars. Can you imagine? He made sixty-two thousand dollars for three weeks' work. My dad never made that in a year. Well, after that first month, things changed. Same briefing, same everything, but everybody left. This happened six days straight. The briefing would be over, and everyone would march out.

"So Sheri came in the next day with this smoking abalone shell and started 'blessing' the office. Now, Mr. Gouldd is from the East Coast like Marc and me. We're born with our arms crossed. So he was rolling his eyes thinking, *Crazy California, land of fruits and nuts.*

"Next briefing, they did over fifteen thousand dollars in sales volume with brand-new people. Record. Next day, Bill Gouldd was walking around with that smoking abalone shell blessing the office.

"Now we do it every morning and every night. It's sage. The Native Americans used it for centuries. It purifies the air and cleanses neg energy. It works, man."

"Is that why everybody is so happy here?"

"It's one reason, man. But the real deal is we're working for ourselves: no boss, no measly limited salary, no glass ceiling. It's unlimited, so it brings out our unlimited human potential. You'll grow so much here, dude. The reason most people are so unhappy is they're so limited that they don't even try. Their bodies are so crammed with toxins from the polluted air, toxic water, and processed chemical foods that they're catatonic. The average American watches seven hours of TV daily, dude. They're just killing time before they die. They've lost the passion, the zest. It's like when you catch a wave just right. You feel like you're connected to everything in the universe. Most people have lost the connection."

"How long have you guys been doing this?"

"Just a short time."

"And you're making money?"

"Dude, the money is unlimited. That's the best part. Unlimited cash." These are the first of many smoothly unanswered questions.

"So how did you guys get started?"

"We bought product. It's the only way. You have to invest in your future. Can you imagine a 7-Eleven with no Twinkies? You've got to have inventory."

"So you guys had money to get started?"

"No, dude. We sold our surfboards. It was like selling my spleen. But Sheri told us the level of our success would depend on the level of our commitment. We're committed."

More people start coming into the office now. The happy party atmosphere is being created again. A buffet of food is set up in the kitchen area, flowers are arranged, and everything is being cleaned and polished. I'm right in the middle of it. I feel like I'm part of something special.

Marc pulls me into a small room and closes the door.

"Rob, do you want to be part of this deal?"

"Yeah."

"Okay. You're no longer a new person. Now you're part of the team. You have to help us create energy. The new people come in, and they're scared and uncomfortable. They're out of their comfort zone. They're skeptical. We have to create an environment where they feel comfortable, where they uncross their arms and open their minds. Most people prejudge before they understand. Didn't it feel good when you first came in here?"

"Yeah. It felt like HappyLand."

"That is by design. We create that. You're either giving energy or you're sucking energy. Most people suck, so we have to give. During the briefing, laugh at the jokes, raise your hand high, sit on the edge of your seat, and don't let your back touch the chair. Give energy to the speaker, lean forward, look in the speaker's eyes, and smile."

"That's like what Casey was doing."

"Casey's the best. She gives energy and drags bodies."

This time the speaker is Chris Mitchel. He used to be a top executive for a major oil company, but he left to do this. He's a handsome, well-dressed, black gentleman. Very professional but monotone.

The energy is definitely lower today. I take it as my personal responsibility to fire up the room. I'm part of the team now. I'm yelling out answers to rhetorical questions. I'm raising my hand as high as I can. I'm laughing loud. He asks for a volunteer, and I jump over the front row of people. Shocked, Chris just looks at me. I figure this is my chance to create energy. I turn to the crowd and yell, "Come on guys, get excited! This is our chance to change our lives. We can save the planet and all be rich!"

I look at Marc for approval, and he's wide-eyed, shaking his head no. I think I've done too much.

After the briefing, Marc pulls me into the little room again.

"Dude, killer enthusiasm, but w-a-a-ay too much. You're like Casey when she first got started. You just need to turn down the volume. It's like this. If you want to convert someone to your religion, don't shave your head and wear orange robes. You have to start at the level they're at and build from there. But it's way better to have too much enthusiasm than none at all. You're going to do great."

I know I messed up. But instead of making me feel stupid, he teaches me something.

We eat the buffet to crumbs and go back into the briefing room. This is it, my first Saturday training. I want to rush out and buy one of those bumper stickers: Millionaire in Training.

I'm learning tons. Gary Henk is teaching us about retailing.

"These filters are not hard to sell. I heard Rob already sold a filter, and today is his first training." Everybody claps. "He's already made money.

Why? Because he made a commitment and took action. Congratulations, Rob." More applause.

No way am I going to tell him I actually lost money.

"What happens sometimes is we get a little resistance and then we quit. Let me tell you why persistence beats resistance. How many of you've seen *The Honeymooner's?*"

Most people raise their hand.

"They didn't have refrigerators back then, did they? They had iceboxes. The iceman would bring a five-gallon block of ice every day to each home. Just like the bottled water man now brings five-gallon bottles of water to each home. But how many of you have your ice delivered today?"

Everybody laughs.

"No, that's silly because a better machine was invented, the refrigerator. Times changed. They used to freeze the ice at a central location and then deliver it. They did that for decades. Why? People were used to it. It was the status quo. People are afraid of change. One day somebody brilliant figures he can take the design for the big central freezer that makes the ice and invent a personal size for each home. First off, the companies that delivered the ice weren't too happy about the idea. Any time there's innovation, the people who are vested in the status quo are going to resist. Some bottled water companies say our filter doesn't work. Why? They're scared.

"One of the many things Bill Gouldd has taught me is to follow the money trail. When someone has a vested interest, they will say and do anything to protect what they see as their livelihood. We are rocking the boat here. We are the innovators. Who do you think made more money: the people delivering ice or the people selling refrigerators?"

"Selling refrigerators," we all respond.

"That's right. You're such a smart group. But let me tell you what happened. The company that invented the refrigerator obviously wanted to sell a lot of them. Problem was, it was hard economic times and people didn't have a lot of disposable income. Credit cards weren't invented yet. So they came up with a plan.

"They would take the icebox in trade for a brand-new refrigerator. People would just have to make payments to the refrigerator company, but the payments would be exactly what they were already paying to the iceman. And in three years, they own the refrigerator free and clear. So they have a much better appliance. It freezes, keeps things really cold, and even has a light. They're out no extra money. Everybody wins. Well, except the iceman. That's one of the things about change. The people who don't adapt suffer. But the people at the leading edge prosper. That's where we are: the leading edge.

"But guess what happened. The refrigerator salesman went out knocking on doors, confident to get a one hundred percent closing ratio. But only twenty-five percent of the people bought it. A full three-quarters of the people said no to a better appliance, no extra cost, and no more payments after three years. The company was shocked. They held meetings. No one could figure out why. Finally they hired a company to interview the thousands of people who didn't buy in order to find out why. The results are fascinating.

"I'm rounding these numbers off for simplicity, but they're pretty accurate. Twenty-five percent of the people didn't understand what the salesperson was talking about, so they said no. Have any of you ever done that when you're a little confused? 'Better safe, than sorry.' 'If it sounds too good to be true, it probably is.' I've actually met people who didn't get involved in our business because they said, 'It sounds too good to be true.' Is that stupid or what? How many of you have heard, 'Now, be realistic?' I'd been realistic my whole life, and I was broke. Reality sucks!" Cheers and applause. This is exciting. I'm with him: *My reality sucks; I just never knew there was another option.*

"Anyway, the first twenty-five percent of the people, once they understood what the salesman had been talking about, once they understood how great a deal it was, they bought it. Some people will say no simply because they're confused. They aren't saying no, they're saying know. They want to know more." He writes that last part on the whiteboard.

"So fifty percent of the people ended up buying a refrigerator. The next twenty-five percent I call the 'status quo people.' They said, 'Pa never had one, Grandpa never had one, and Great Grandpa never had one, so why do I need one?' They resist change. Innovation scares them. These people will only buy a water filter when all of their neighbors have one. Because now the status quo is to have one rather than not. They'll be sitting around the dinner table one night and say, 'The Joneses just bought one of them new-fangled water filters. Everybody seems to be getting 'em. They're talking about the toxins in the water and all. I think maybe we should get one, too. That growth on little Suzy's neck is getting bigger.' " Everybody laughs at that.

"The last twenty-five percent are the people who say, 'What's an icebox?' They're the stupid people. Let them drink chlorine. One guy came up to me and said in a backwoods accent, 'If chlorine wasn't good fer ya, the government wouldn't put it in the water. You know what else I found out? My brother's also my dad.' " The crowd is rolling now. Talk about getting the energy going.

"So if people don't buy your filter on the first try, maybe they didn't understand you, maybe they're in the status quo and we'll sell them later, and maybe they're stupid." I'm glad my mom bought one the first time.

"All I know is that over fifty percent of the homes in America are going to have a water filtration system by nineteen ninety-five. Right now less than five percent of the homes have filters. That means about one hundred million homes are going to buy a water filter in the next five years. It'll be the biggest marketing trend in history. And we're at the cutting edge."

I suddenly realize I'm going to be rich!

Often people attempt to live their lives backward; they try to have more things, or more money, in order to do more of what they want, so they will be happier. The way it actually works is in reverse. You must first be who you really are, then do what you need to do, in order to have what you want.

Margaret Young

Chapter 5

You can't cross the sea merely by staring at the water.
Rabindranath Tagore

By Monday, I cover the check I wrote to Seth. This is the first of many "just barely" money adventures. I've quit my teaching job and am having some success in selling my filters, mostly at cost. I'm such a wimp when it comes to money. As soon as I get any sales resistance, I crumble.

"Here, you can have it at my cost. I'm not making a dime. Look, here's my receipt. I just want you and your family to have pure water." I'd also like to make some money, but I figure this is part of the learning curve. I "sell" all of my filters just in time for the "close of the month," the time when we have to make sure we are "in position."

"You're going to get qualified Manager, aren't you, Rob?" Marc has taken me under his wing.

"I don't have the money. I would love to, but there's no way."

"There's always a way. How's your credit?"

"Not an option."

"On the East Coast we have a special bank. I'm not sure if you guys have it out here. It's called Bank of Mom."

"That branch is closed for me. She thinks I joined a cult."

"You never know. It can't hurt to ask. You sold all of your filters, right?"

"Yeah." I never tell anyone I "sell" them at cost.

Marc continues, "So you can already show profit, and you're just getting started. You've got to be at least a Manager, because then you'll make a percentage on all the people you sign up next month. If you're just a Dealer, you only make money when you personally sell. Dude, the big money is in Manager and above. Hold on, let me ask Sheri something." He runs off.

I have not signed up one person in three weeks. Since I quit my teaching job, I have been in the office fourteen to eighteen hours a day. I'm learning a lot. Everybody keeps telling me how great I am and how wonderful I'm doing, but I've done nothing. I raise my hand and laugh during the briefings. I help keep the office clean and cue the videotapes. But I'm not signing anybody up.

Marc comes back obviously excited, "Dude, you're not even going to believe this. I can't even believe this. Sheri really likes you, man. She thinks you have what it takes. Check this out. She said that if you can find a way to come up with five thousand dollars, she's going to give you ten thousand dollars in excess volume and make you not just a Manager, but a Car Qualified for next month. You're in, man. This is awesome."

"What's excess volume?"

"Dude, Sheri does so much volume in her group that she has excess that she can give to people she really believes in, but it's just a limited amount."

"Well, could she give me the whole fifteen thousand dollars of excess volume, and I'll sign a contract that as soon as I start making money, I'll pay her back with interest?"

"Doesn't work that way, man. You've got to make a commitment. You'll never get to second base if you're afraid to take your foot off first." His reference to first and second base makes me think of dating in high school. He continues, "If somebody gives you something, it doesn't have the same value as if you struggled for it. If Bill Gouldd gave you a million dollars, you'd have money, but you wouldn't have the self-satisfaction of earning it, of fighting for it. It's not what you have; it's who you become in the process of getting that matters. Sheri's doing it for you, man—your future. She believes in you. Don't let her down."

"Mom, I'm just going to tell you straight. I need five thousand dollars to get my business started."

"Now, Rob, you've spent the last three weeks wasting your time. You have not brought in any money, and now you want us to give you more money that you can throw away. No. End of conversation."

"You haven't even heard why. What if I told you that if you give me five thousand dollars, I'm going to get ten thousand more given to me guaranteed?"

"What are you talking about?"

"Sheri Sharman believes in me. If I can come up with five thousand dollars, she is going to give me ten thousand extra so I can be a Car Qualified and not just a Manager."

"They're going to give you ten thousand dollars and a car if you can come up with five thousand dollars? Can you get that in writing?"

"Well, I don't actually get a car. I'm just called a "Car Qualified." It's a higher position in the marketing plan where I get more percentages. I get an extra ten percent on my whole sales force."

"Ten percent of nothing is nothing."

"Mom, I'm just getting started. Think if you had given up on me during my first three weeks of walking. I never would have gotten a track scholarship for college. I paid for my own education. Help me now. This is my chance. I know I can do it."

"Five thousand dollars is a lot of money."

We sit down with Doug, my step-dad, and they decide to co-sign a bank loan for me. I get a loan for $6,500 to cover tax and shipping and other expenses in getting started. I'm in business.

I get my order in the last day of the month. Everybody is excited, especially Dawn. I'm a Car Qualified now.

I'm practically skipping along the hall when Sheri calls me into her office.

"Close the door, Rob. I have something I want to show you."

She hands me three magazines: *Inc., Fortune,* and *Success.* Some of the pages are marked with paper clips.

"Go ahead, turn to the marked pages. What do you see?"

"A man in a suit." I'm confused and nervous.

"What does the man look like?"

I'm praying I don't say something stupid. "A successful businessman?"

"Good, now go on to the next one. What does he look like?"

I figure it worked the last time, so I'll try it again. "A successful businessman."

"Good, now look at the next one."

We look through about fifteen photos. They all look like successful businessmen.

"Do you see a pattern?"

"Yeah, they're all successful businessmen."

"What else?"

"They are all well-dressed."

"What else?"

"They're all wearing ties?"

"Facial hair, Rob. What about their facial hair?"

I flip back through the pictures. "They don't have any."

"Exactly. Now look in that mirror. What do you see?"

Whenever I'm uncomfortable I try to make a joke. "A Woodstock revivalist."

She laughs. "And what do you want to be?"

"A successful businessman."

"Great. I'll see you tomorrow, Rob."

She doesn't say it, but there's no doubt in my mind that she wants to see me clean-shaven tomorrow. I typically rebel against people telling me what to do, but because she hasn't told me, I can't rebel.

I get so many compliments the next day on my clean-shaven face that it's embarrassing. Marina starts to join me at the office now. We're building our future together.

Everybody is excited about the upcoming big training in Salt Lake City. This will be my first "Basic Building Blocks to Success" seminar. I want to go. I want to go badly. But there's no money.

"Dude, are you jacked about this weekend or what?" Joe is always excited.

"Bud, I want to go so bad."

"What do you mean, 'want to go'?"

"I've got *no* money."

"Whoa. Lack thought. Neg police, arrest this man. Are you kidding me? You've got a chance to learn directly from the master, no whisper down the lane, and you're worried about a few hundred bucks? Dude, take a reality check. Remember what the man always says, 'If you can't afford to, you can't afford not to.' "

"I know. I know. Believe me, I know I need to be there. I just have to figure out a way."

"Damn right you do. You've already spent thousands of dollars on your business for inventory, and you're crying about a few hundred bucks to get trained on how to sell it. I'm surprised at you. This is the one piece that is missing in your personal puzzle of success. You're going to come back a focused, money-making machine."

"Do they have a courtesy credit plan like when I first bought product so that I can go? Then when I make all the money, I'll pay them back."

"No way, man. You've got to find a way. I don't care what you have to do. Find a way. When we're gazillionaires we'll be laughing about all this. Right now we're just building stories that will give spice to our riches. It's like Bill Gouldd says: 'If you don't think your future is worth three hundred dollars, I don't either.' You need training. It's the difference between a mass murderer and a brain surgeon, dude. They both use a knife but with totally different results. Sheri and Mr. Gouldd both use the same marketing plan you do, but you're broke while they're making millions. Why? Training, bro, training. This weekend is make it or break it for you. You're either going to take off like a rocket ship or get left behind. There are three types of people in this world: those who make things happen—they take action and risks, and they get the babe and the red Lamborghini; those who contemplate, consider, and evaluate what's going to happen; and those who say, 'What happened?' "

I'm going. I figure it is fate that it's in Salt Lake City. I can stay with my Uncle Morgan and save on hotel costs. I have to sell my stereo and my mountain bike, but I've got enough money to pay the $300 for the seminar and cover gas and travel expenses.

The fresh air of Pegasus is invigorating in San Diego, but it's freezing in Utah. I finally close the window, figuring that if the door rattles off, I'm just building stories.

I get to Uncle Morgan's house tired and excited. He's not as excited as I am. "Rob, here in Utah we've seen so many of these companies come and go. This area is the sacred breeding ground for multilevel companies. Some people have made a lot of money. But many more people have lost money and been hurt, some devastated. I just want to make sure you're going in with your eyes open." Uncle Morgan is concerned, but he is also friendly and ultimately encouraging. He's had his share of wild hairs in his life, and he can tell how excited I am.

Friday night there's a briefing for the new people. Uncle Morgan does not come, so I have no distractions. I get to focus completely on the master's message.

Mr. Gouldd starts speaking:

"The system is designed for and by the capitalists, the creators, the innovators, the risk takers. But our educational system trains us how to be employees, followers. Why? Because the capitalists need us to work in their factories, to work their farms, to do the things that have to be done to make the system function. But it is work they will not do because it holds no promise of residual income or financial freedom. If you live in a capitalist country like the United States of America, and you are not a capitalist, *you have no capital.*" Though there are hundreds of people in the room, it feels like he is talking only to me.

"Over ninety percent of the people who reach sixty-five are dependent on friends, family, or the federal government just to survive. More people have a net worth of one hundred dollars or more at the age of twenty than they do at sixty-five. These people dedicated forty years of their lives to building equity in someone else's company. And when they're too old to work anymore, they're given a watch and retired on half of the income they could not live on before. Not because the company is concerned and wants them to enjoy their golden years. It's because they don't want them to die at their desk."

I'm driving back to Uncle Morgan's angry, agitated, and excited. Why didn't I learn this stuff in college? Obviously, the system needs more workers. They wanted me to be an employee and support the system they created for themselves. Thank God I learned this at twenty-five instead of sixty-five like most people. Now that I know the rules, I can play the game.

I wake up early, eat fast, drive the hour to Salt Lake City, and arrive at the seminar before 7 A.M. so that I can help as "staff." I'm not quite sure what being on staff means. I do know I still have to pay $300.

It turns out I was supposed to arrive at 6 A.M. They changed the time. Imo gives me the evil eye. Imo is Sheri Sharman's mom and can be very sweet, but don't piss her off and don't be late. She runs the logistics of the seminars and protects the company, Bill Gouldd, and her daughter like a tigress. Because this is my first seminar, she withholds "the wrath of Imo."

We get all of the chairs in perfect rows, blow up hundreds of balloons, and make everything to Bill Gouldd's exacting standards. This is only my first seminar, but I'm on the inside. As we are setting up, I hear the story of how it all started.

When Sheri first met Bill Gouldd, he was broke and homeless with no car. They were meeting in a Bennigan's restaurant. Sheri's friend had invited her to learn about a business opportunity. Bill Gould was the closer. As soon as he saw Sheri, he told her friend to cancel the next two appointments and to leave them alone.

They talked for three hours.

"What are your dreams, Sheri?"

"Paying my bills seems like a dream right now."

"Let's say all your bills are taken care of. You have extra money, lots of it. What would you like to do, for you?"

"I would like to move into a nicer neighborhood and get a new car."

"What kind of car?" he asked, building the dream.

"How much money do I have?"

"As much as you need, as much as you want."

"A Mercedes." She felt silly and excited saying it.

"What color?"

"Black."

"What color leather?"

"Black."

"How do you think you'll feel parking that black-on-black, brand-new Mercedes-Benz in the driveway of your new home?" He didn't give her time to answer. "What kind of home will you have, Sheri?"

"An ocean view. No, right on the ocean, with dolphins playing in my backyard. It has pastel colors and huge windows, and the ocean is my backyard." She was visibly excited then. It was time for the close.

"Sheri, I can show you how to have all of this. We're going to build this business together. I'll teach you. I'll train you."

"No." Fear blurred Sheri's vision. "I cannot do sales. I have friends who have tried things like this, and they all lost money. I have no money to lose. I can't."

Rather than pushing against resistance, he changed course.

"Okay, if it's not for you, it's not for you."

She relaxed.

"Obviously, you are content with what you're doing. But could you do me a favor?"

"Sure." She was starting to like him, but her guard was up.

"I have to go to Orange County tomorrow for a meeting with this company. Could you give me a ride?"

"Sure."

As fate would have it, during the meeting in Orange County, one of Sheri's girlfriends walked across the stage and gave a testimonial.

"I am not sure how, but I made eight thousand dollars last month sharing these incredible products with my friends."

Sheri looked over at Bill. "I'm doing this," she decided.

Imo had given Sheri an emergency credit card; Sheri considered this an emergency. They ordered $5,000 worth of water filters on Imo's Visa.

One week later, Imo called Sheri.

"Sheri, I just got a call from my credit card company."

"I know, Mom. I was meaning to call you."

"What's going on?"

"Well, I met this man at a restaurant. He showed me that if I bought five thousand dollars worth of water filters, I could get rich."

"Who is this man, Sheri?"

"His name is Bill Gould."

"How old is he?"

"Thirty-three."

"What does he do for a living?"

"He sells water filters."

"Where does he live?"

"With me."

"Why doesn't he live in his own house?"

"His parents kicked him out."

"What kind of car does he drive?"

"Mine."

Imo was not impressed with Bill Gould or his track record.

"Sheri, if he is such a great businessman, why doesn't he have any money? Why was he living at his parent's house? Why doesn't he have a car? Why doesn't he have any business partners or friends he could live with? You just met him! Why is he living at your house and driving your car and charging my credit card?"

Sheri was quiet. She didn't know how to respond. This was her chance. It wasn't logical, and she did not want logic to cloud her dream. The master had closed the sale. . . . She was spellbound.

As soon as he had met Sheri, Bill Gould knew he'd found what he'd been looking for, what he'd needed, what he'd been missing—a buffer. A sweet, innocent, caring angel who could build rapport with a prospective audience before he closed them. His intensity blew people out or in. One hundred percent commitment, dedication, and sacrifice—or hit the road. They used to call him M. M., "Maniac on a Mission." He even put it on his business cards: Bill Gould, M. M.

That was before he changed the spelling of his name to end with two Ds. In 1988, soon after he met Sheri, a numerologist told him that his name was out of balance. If he added another D, she said, the universe would bring him abundance.

Look at the results.

Imo was not happy about the maniac who had just recruited her daughter to his mission. But eighteen months later, when Sheri pulled up in a brand-new, black-on-black Mercedes-Benz, Imo re-evaluated. She became the most dedicated person in the company.

At 9 A.M., the music starts, and we let in all of the new people. People are dancing. The energy is rocking. The song "I Want to Be Rich" is playing. A group of girls have changed the chorus. They're screaming and giggling, "I want to do Rich." Rich Von is one of the top people. The girls are cute. I consider changing my name.

It's now ten o'clock, and I start looking at my watch wondering what is going on. The seminar is supposed to start at nine. I'm having fun dancing, but $300 is a pretty steep cover charge.

"Marc, is everything okay?"

"What do you mean?"

"I mean it's ten o'clock. The seminar was supposed to start at nine."

"Never question The Man. He'll start when it's time. Everything he does has a reason."

For some reason that doesn't comfort me. I start calculating in my head. I paid $300. He's probably going to talk about seven or eight hours a day. So I'm paying about twenty dollars an hour to hear him speak. He's an hour late. I just lost $20. I suddenly don't feel like dancing.

Finally, just past 11 A.M., the music stops. Because I'm on staff, I have a great seat in the second row. Membership has its privileges.

He comes walking out in a baseball uniform. Everybody goes wild. Standing ovation. Whistles and cheers. I feel like I'm at a rock concert.

"What does a baseball player need?" We can hardly hear him over the cheers. We take our seats.

"What does a baseball player need?"

One guy across the row yells out, "A bat."

Another yells, "A mitt."

A girl yells, "A ball."

I want to say a field to play on, but I'm afraid I'll stutter. Whenever I'm excited and nervous, I make a joke.

I yell out, "Chewing tobacco."

He stops, slowly turns, and looks straight at me. I freeze halfway through a breath.

"Some of you guys wonder why you're not making any money yet. You bring fucking idiots like this to my seminar. How the fuck do you expect to make any money when you're working with assholes like this? And how the hell did you get a seat in the second row?" I look at him like a deer in the headlights. He continues the seminar. I breathe in.

"A baseball player needs a team and a coach. I'm the coach, and you are the team."

People seem to move away from me. I remember a dream I used to have in which I'd get to school only to realize I had forgotten to put my pants on, and everybody would be laughing at me. Why hadn't I just kept my mouth shut? Why did I have to be a smart-ass?

At the lunch break I eat alone; people seem to avoid me. I can't find Seth, or Marc, or Joe. I don't really look. I deserve to be alone.

A woman who sits to my right surprises me. "Don't worry about it. He'll forget about it. When he's on stage, he's just laser focused. You got zapped, that's all. Just don't do it again." No worries there. I look at her and smile. I feel better.

The rest of the day is amazing. He talks until 2 A.M. He creates a new organization within the company to recognize the top leaders, the Round Table. Six people become its founding members: Sheri Sharman, Rich Von, Lori Rubidge, Marc Accetta, Ricky Frank, and Ken McKenny. Bill Gouldd leads us in a verbal commitment that one day we, too, are going to be "Knights of the Round Table."

It's 3 A.M., and I have to be ready for staff at 6 A.M. I decide to sleep in my car. I have done it before, but in San Diego. It's cold in Utah. I'm shivering so violently that I begin to worry about hypothermia. It is a big hotel, so I find a secluded hallway and curl up to sleep.

I'm up before my alarm. I go in the bathroom and my hair looks like Buckwheat's from the Lil' Rascals. All of my stuff is at Uncle Morgan's, so I strip down to my waist and shampoo my hair in the sink with the hand soap from the dispenser. In fifteen minutes, I'm ready to go. I get down to the seminar room a half-hour early. Imo smiles.

Day two is even more amazing. By 5 P.M. I'm "brain dead," another company phrase also known as "brain overload." Mr. Gouldd keeps talking until well after midnight. Logically I should rest at Uncle Morgan's and then drive home. But this is not a logical company. It's emotional and I'm excited. I stop to grab my stuff, leave a note, and start driving. I'm not even tired. In fact, I feel more awake and alive than I can remember. I don't even go home. I drive eight hours straight to the office. I'm the first one there, even before Marc and Joe. The cleaning people let me in. Speaking Spanish has advantages.

It feels strange to be in the office alone. I look at the glass case filled with rhinos and run my hand along Sheri's desk. I take several deep breaths and begin to create my future. I have less money than I did on Friday, but I've never felt so wealthy.

My enthusiasm carries me through the next two weeks. Last Friday there was a meeting just for "deskholders" that I couldn't attend because I was only a "part-timer." I had stared at those closed double wooden doors and decided I would never be on the outside again, and I learned my first lesson in the "fear of loss" sales technique: Most people are more motivated by fear of loss than they are by desire for gain, so don't sell them on what they will get if they buy, sell them on what they'll miss if they don't.

I rent a desk for $500 a month and pay for my own phone line and ads. I'm spending the last of the money I got from the loan, but now I'm a deskholder—I'm on the inside.

The office is bursting with excitement because Bill Gouldd is coming on Wednesday night. He's been on the East Coast opening offices. This will be the first time I've seen him since Salt Lake City.

People have been calling my ads, and I have been booking them all for Wednesday night to see Mr. Gouldd. From what I've heard, everybody he talks to signs up. I know nobody I've talked to has signed up, so I figure I'll let the Big Guy talk to them. That's what some of us call him. Bill Gouldd, Big Guy, B. G. We have a whole language that unites us and confuses the new people.

It's the big night. Bill Gouldd is coming. I'm so excited. I walk in the bathroom, and there he is, just standing there, peeing in the urinal.

"Mr. Gouldd, H . . . H . . . Hi. I . . . I'm Rob Styler. It's a pleasure to meet you in person." I'm hoping he doesn't remember I'm the guy he yelled at in Salt Lake City. I put out my hand to shake his. He looks at my hand, looks at the urinal, and looks back at me. This is the second of many times I do the stupidest thing possible in his presence. I feel like an idiot.

I turn to walk out and he says, "Did you come in here for some reason, or did you just want to shake my hand while I'm peeing?" Man, I figure he already thinks I'm an idiot, but he'll think I'm a spineless idiot if I walk out.

I go over to the urinal, and he starts to wash his hands. I can't pee. I'm just staring at the wall hoping he isn't listening. Hoping he doesn't notice that my bladder is as scared as I am. I am thankful when he begins to talk.

"You seem real excited. Are you always like this?"

"I . . . I . . . I just got nervous meeting you. And, well, I'm also excited because I have twenty-six people coming to see you tonight. I heard everybody you talk to signs up. I'm just getting started, but I'm a Car Qualified."

"Congratulations, you're going to do great." He walks out. I can pee.

I go over to the sink and there's his jewelry, just sitting there. It is all gold and diamonds—big diamonds, huge diamonds. I pick up the ring and look at the diamond. It's heavy in my hand. The watch is a solid gold Rolex with diamonds everywhere. One link on this watch is worth more than Pegasus. I've got to get these back to him. I pick up both rings and the watch and carry them like quail eggs.

"H . . . H . . . Here's your stuff, Mr. Gouldd."

"Wow, thanks! I can't believe I did that. What a day."

I'm waiting for my people to show up. They still have twenty minutes before the meeting starts. There must be a lot of traffic. I told them to be here early. Twenty minutes come and go. Mr. Gouldd waits a while for everybody to get seated. There are about three hundred people in the room. We use the big room downstairs for events like this. It used to be a church, so we cover up the cross with a banner.

I've put everything I have into this night. I've spent all my money on ads. I had it all figured out. If twenty-six people come, and they all start as Managers with $5,000 after hearing Mr. Gouldd, I am going to get a check for over $40,000 and I will become a "Fifth Dimension," just one level beneath Mr. Gouldd and Sheri. This is the night my business is going to "go to the next level." The momentum is supposed to start tonight. But how is the momentum going to start when nobody shows up?

Dejected, I sit near the back of the room. Casey calls to me excitedly.

"Rob, one of your guests is here." I'm so depressed I don't even get up. I just motion for him to come over and sit by me. He hand signals that he is fine where he is, and that's fine by me.

What am I going to do? I have no more money. I owe my parents $6,500. My product hasn't even come yet. I'm so consumed in my little world of fear that I hardly hear Mr. Gouldd's message.

When he finishes to a standing ovation, I turn around. My guest has left. It's just as well, because I don't know what I'd say to him anyway. "Follow me! You, too, can go broke in thirty days."

Sheri calls me over. "Where are your new people? I want to talk to them."

"Only one guy came and he left already. Sheri, I had twenty-six people booked and confirmed for tonight."

"Ad calls, right?"

"Yeah."

"You can't wait to invite your ad calls to the big event. You invite them down to a briefing as soon as they call the ad. Get them excited about the big event and then they can invite their 'warm market' for you. Remember other people's efforts. You're still trying to do it all yourself, silly. Also, people have short memories and even shorter attention spans. If they called your ad over forty-eight hours ago, they've already forgotten about it." Now she tells me. "It's okay, Rob, you're learning."

I'm going to be starving pretty soon, too.

Most of the new people have left, and we've packed up the chairs. I drag myself into the bathroom and as fate would have it, there's Mr. Gouldd again. I want to walk back out, but he sees me.

"Are you following me?" he says with a smile. "Hey, thanks again for the jewelry." He looks at me closer. "What happened? You look like someone barbecued your dog. You're not the same hyper-man I met in here a few hours ago."

"R . . . R . . . Remember I told you I had twenty-six people coming to see you tonight?"

"Yeah."

"Only one showed up."

"What happened with that one?"

"I was so depressed I hardly even talked to him."

He looks at me like I am gum on the bottom of his shoe. "You mean you had a prospect here tonight who heard me speak and you didn't even talk to him. You focused on what you didn't have rather than what you did." He shakes his head in disgust. "Remember when I told you earlier that you are going to do great?"

"Y . . . Yeah."

"I take it back. You've got the wrong attitude." He walks out.

I study the grout on the floor tile then leave, forgetting to pee.

I learn several things: Invite people right away to the office and let them invite their friends. Remember to use other people's efforts. Don't wait for the big event. Focus on what I have, instead of what I don't have. And don't try to pee when Mr. Gouldd is in the bathroom.

Money can't buy happiness—but then, happiness can't buy groceries.
Unknown

Chapter 6

It is difficult to satisfy one's appetite by painting pictures of cakes.
Unknown

I'm back in the office at 7:30 A.M. Marc and Joe are the only ones here. They always seem to be here.

"Wasn't Bill Gouldd amazing last night?" Joe is excited. "My people freaked. They were blown away, dude. All I had to say was, 'Here's your pen. Here's your order. Fill it out.'"

Marc agrees, "Volume was pumping. Everybody was doing orders." They can see I'm not as excited as they are.

"Oh, dude, I'm sorry. I heard you got skunked," Joe winces.

"It's okay man, learning lesson," Marc says.

"Yeah, I learned a lot," I say with a sigh. "I was depressed last night. But, heck, I've only been doing this a month. Anything worthwhile takes time. I'm paying my dues."

"Does this guy have the killer attitude or what? High five on that." We slap hands. "The man gets skunked at the big event and he's here at 7:30 A.M. the next morning. You're just building stories, man. When we're millionaires racing our Lear Jets, we're going to laugh about these hard times." *Marc's great.*

"I just hope I can survive till then," I say while looking at the ground.

"What do you mean?"

"I mean, I've got no money."

"Dude, never say that in the office. Sheri would freak if she heard you say that. Remember, no neg energy in the office. That's why we sage."

"Don't you have product?" Joe joins the conversation.

"Yeah, it just came yesterday," I respond.

"Man, you're crying broke when you've got $7,500 dollars sitting in your garage." Joe looks at me. "All you have to do is sell it. Get off your ass and sell some product. In fact, get out of the office today. Go retail. You're giving me the willies. You'll feel better when you have some cash in your pocket."

I drive out of the parking lot confused. I've spent almost every waking hour of the last month in the office. It is my cocoon, the only safe place where I feel good about what I'm doing.

The fresh air of Pegasus again inspires me. I'm going to retail.

"Marina, we have to sell some of these filters to get some money," I say in Spanish.

"Rob, you go. I don't want to."

"Come on. Remember, we decided we're a team."

"I can't even speak English. It takes me fifteen minutes to explain simple things to your mom and step-dad."

"We'll go to a Spanish-speaking area of San Diego." This excites her because I know she misses her culture.

We put all forty filters in the trunk of Pegasus and decide we're not coming home until at least half are sold.

We stop at Taco Bell to eat something. We reread the section in the manual about retailing. We get gas. We drive around looking for the "right neighborhood." We're both scared.

Finally, I just park. "We're going up to that green door right there."

I get the filter and test kit out of the trunk, and we walk up the driveway. I knock. An older Spanish woman answers the door.

"D . . . D . . . Disculpe p . . . p . . . pero . . . " She looks over at Marina for help. My Spanish isn't bad, but sometimes I stutter so much that people think I can't speak the language.

Marina saves us and, before I know it, we're invited in. The woman is from Guatemala and has the same name as Marina's mother, Magdelena. I'm feeling good about this. We are building rapport. That was the first part in the manual on retailing. I can feel a sale.

They keep talking and talking. I'm waiting for Marina to turn the conversation toward the filter, but she's having too much fun talking. She's so starved for her culture that our retailing adventure is becoming a cathartic experience for her. It's been over an hour now. I decide to take action and ask for a glass of water. She pours me a glass of bottled water.

"You use bottled water?"

"*Si, señor*, the water from the tap tastes awful."

"I know, but bottled water is so expensive."

"Si."

"What if I could get you better than bottled-quality water for two cents a gallon?"

"What?" She looks over at Marina who nods yes.

"Here, let me show you." I hook up the filter and then do the water test, turning the tap water yellow while the filtered water stays clear. She's amazed. She calls out and suddenly there are ten people in the kitchen all talking in Spanish so quickly that I can barely understand any of them. I do note that the father is not excited. He keeps talking about no money and how he's been drinking the tap water for years. Apparently, the bottled water is just for children and guests.

I'm talking some more with Magdelena. When I reach to show her the yellow water again, the glass is empty. I look around, confused.

"I drank it," the father says proudly.

"You drank it!" I can't believe this. The chemical used to test the water is highly corrosive. It is part hydrochloric acid. My first real sales attempt and I'll probably be charged with manslaughter. "Here, drink this quick." I reach in their refrigerator and give him milk. I read once that milk neutralizes acids.

Everybody is scared now because they can tell I'm scared. The children are crying. Magdelena is praying. One son is calling the doctor. Another son is running to find the neighbor who's a nurse. The father finishes his milk and is sitting on the couch trying to figure out if he's dying. Marina's comforting Magdelena and I'm trying to be calm because I'm scaring everyone.

"Okay, relax. There were just a few drops in the water. It's probably nothing." We spend about another hour comforting everyone. The father is fine.

Magdelena wants the filter, but he insists they have no money. National Safety Associates recommends using "the puppy dog approach"— leave the filter with the family for a few days and they'll never want to part with it. I owe them at least a free filter for a few days since I almost killed their father. Who knows, maybe they'll buy it.

As we're leaving, Marina is smart enough to ask if they know anyone who might be interested in a filter.

"Oh, yes. My sister across the street, my brother next door, my friend right over there." She points to a smaller house at the end of the street. "But I am going to call them first and tell them not to drink the yellow water." We all laugh. "Just tell them Magdelena sent you. *Adios*, Marina."

We have installed our first filter and gotten three leads. I'm looking at what I have, rather than what I don't have, which is no more money than this morning when we started.

We install seven more filters and get a bunch more leads. No sales. Finally at 9 P.M. we head home, tired.

Three days later I call the phone numbers the people gave me where we left the filters. Five are disconnected and three just ring with no answering machine. One week passes. Two weeks. A month. There's always some excuse why I can't drive back to that neighborhood. I never go back to those eight homes. I don't feel bad about it. I figure eight families in National City are drinking better water for free.

It's right before the briefing and I'm talking with Dawn and Seth in the kitchen area of the office. I hear his voice: "WHERE DID YOU GET THAT?" Bill Gouldd is marching across the room straight at me with his finger pointing at my chest.

"W . . . W . . . What?" I'm petrified. *What did I do?*

"That." He's still pointing at my chest.

I lift my tie. "M . . . My mom bought it for me."

"Not your tie, stupid. That pin. That rhino pin—where did you get it?"

"My sister gave it to me when she found out our company symbol is the rhino."

"Where did she get it?"

"I don't know."

"Call her."

As fate would have it, my sister Kendra is best friends with Yvette, who is the fiancé of Richard Burnett, an old partner of Bill Gouldd. They had made matching rhino pins ten years ago. Yvette had given the pin to my sister. Mr. Gouldd had lost his five years ago. He borrows mine to make a mold. What are the odds? Again the universe is proving I'm on the right path.

The next day I'm in the office early. I often beat Marc and Joe now. I hear the front door open. Sheri Sharman walks into the back office.

"Rob, when I pulled up and saw your car, I just smiled. You're such a hard worker. I want to work with you more directly. What are you doing?"

"Just waiting for the phone to ring."

"Let me see the ads you have in this week."

"Well, Sheri, I ran out of credit at the newspaper and I don't have any money, so I don't have any ads this week."

"But you're waiting for the phone to ring?" She is half confused, half angry. "Who's going to call you, your mom? That's like fishing with no hook. You need to go out and meet some people. You need to go recruit."

She sends me to the mall to recruit some people. It's before 8 A.M., so nobody's there yet. I have two hours to rehash childhood fears. Ever since I first started to talk, I have stuttered. I still blame my brother. When I was learning to talk, he was my role model and he stuttered. He stopped, I continued.

Kids are brutally honest. If you're fat, they tell you, repeatedly. If you're not good at sports, they fight over who has to have you on their team. I had always wanted to make friends, but in everything besides sports, I was painfully shy. My stuttering hadn't helped. I would approach a kid on the playground, "H . . . Hi, I'm R . . . R . . . Ro . . . Ro . . . Ro . . . Robby." He would look at me and say, "Hi, R . . . R . . . Ro . . . Ro . . . Ro . . . Robby. Hey, come here guys, this kid can't talk." I would laugh along because I wanted to be accepted, but inside it hurt. It formed much of my personality.

Before meeting Bill Gouldd, I'd just wanted to have my organic farm in Guatemala and not have much contact with society. Now, on a daily basis, I'm surrounded by strangers, and today I have to walk around a mall, approach people I've never met, and recruit them. I feel nauseous. I venture from the safety of Pegasus and begin to stalk the mall. I take a strategic position where I can see but not be seen.

People walk innocently by. I wait for the right person, the future leader of my sales force. I see one. I take three tentative steps forward. No, I don't like his shoes. I'll wait. Maybe her? No, she looks stuck up. Nobody's quite right. I spend four hours, and not one person is right.

I go back to the office. Sheri sees me. "Okay, where's your list of recruits? I'm going to help you call them back."

"Sheri, nobody was right."

"What do mean, nobody was right?" she says with a tone.

"I mean nobody had the look. They weren't leaders, and I need leaders in my group."

"Come here." She's mad, but Sheri has a strong nurturing side to her. We go into her office. She closes the door.

"You were scared, weren't you?"

"No," I say defensively.

"How long are you going to let your fears stand in the way of your dreams?"

"I'm not scared."

"Rob, you're trying to build a people business, and you're afraid to talk to one person."

I take a deep breath through my nostrils. "It's my stuttering. I'm afraid that when I talk to them, I'm going to stutter and I'll lose credibility."

"Rob, when you respect yourself, others will respect you. How did you feel driving back to the office not having talked to one person in four hours? Did you feel proud?"

"No."

"You have to go back there and talk to one person. Not ten like the goal we originally set, just one. Can you do that?"

"Yes." I feel a surge of confidence and literally run to the car.

I'm going to talk to the first person I see. I park Pegasus and head straight for a well-dressed woman in her forties. I walk right up to her, put out my hand, open my mouth, and nothing comes out, not a sound. She kindly shakes my hand and looks at me expectantly. I stare blankly at her. Not a sound will leave my throat. Not a sound, not a stutter.

I turn and run. I'm twenty-six years old, running through the mall. I take a seat on a secluded bench and swallow deep breaths. *Okay, okay, that didn't count because, well, because I didn't talk. I'll do better next time. One person, that's all I have to do.*

Before I have time to talk myself out of it, I head straight for a woman in her fifties. I put out my hand, open my mouth and sounds come out but no words. I squeak and gag. She looks at me and then smiles, reaches in her purse, and hands me a quarter. A quarter!

I hold the quarter up to my face in disbelief. I turn around and begin to laugh, a deep belly laugh. I can't stop. Here I am trying to build my multimillion-dollar business, and this lady hands me a quarter. It's a cathartic laugh. It changes my life.

I've been more concerned about what other people think of me than what I truly want, more concerned about their opinion than my own. When she hands me the quarter, it becomes painfully obvious that I've become like my father, living to please others.

There is a story my father told me the night before he died. He hadn't been able to remember it until that night; he hadn't been able to die until he remembered it.

I was sitting by my father's hospital bed. He was staring straight ahead, speaking slowly.

"Rob, I was just your age . . . We were frightened, just kids." His voice sounded small. He kept pausing to gain strength. "Hitler was desperate. When there was no hope, he ordered the youths—the children—to fight. Our commander was a good man, though, so he told us all to hide in our homes until it was over. We ran, but they caught many of us." His body began to shake. "I didn't help him—he was my best friend but I stayed hidden behind the rock and watched the SS hang him for desertion. My own people hung a thirteen-year-old boy for being afraid." My father looked at me, his eyes clear.

"Son, I think I must have gone mad. I ran wildly through the battle, throwing my grenades in all directions. I wanted to blow it all up, destroy everything.

"Then it was daytime. I was in a cot in a POW camp. My leg was bloody but bandaged."

My father looked at the white curtain surrounding us, the tubes running in and out of his body and his leg, again bloody and bandaged.

"I didn't tell anyone I was German when I came to America. I eradicated my accent. I didn't even tell your mother. I thought she would have nothing to do with me if she knew my past, if she knew what I'd witnessed. A week before our wedding I told her how I'd watched my mentor beaten to death. He was Jewish. They made us each spit on him.

"After I told your mother this story, I walked out of the room. I wanted to make it easier for her to change her mind about marrying me. Lucky for both of us, she didn't." He smiled and even laughed softly. It was strange seeing my father laugh.

I began to cry quietly as he finally shared with me why I'd never understood him, why he'd seemed to live behind a veil. By trying to shield me from his pain, he had kept me from his love. At fourteen, I was shaken as my father laughed with me and cried with me for the first time. He died the next day.

He had permitted little joy in his life. He'd felt undeserving of all his successes. His intellect, his U.S. citizenship, his family—in none of them had he felt pride, only obligation.

It's funny how we become what we most try to avoid. That night I had vowed never to live like my father, and here I am, living to please others, repeating the legacy.

Before going back to the office, I recruit one person.

The last of human freedoms is to choose one's attitude in any given set of circumstances.

Victor Frankl

Chapter 7

Ah, but a man's reach should exceed his grasp, or what's a heaven for?
Robert Browning

Bill Gouldd drives up in his tricked-out 280Z. We all press against the window and watch. His license plate reads Z Rhino. Our company symbol is the rhino: a thick-skinned, powerful animal with mythical characteristics that is naturally gentle and independent. But if anybody pisses it off, it can run thirty miles an hour and stick a horn anywhere it wants.

He walks in the building and goes to the office next door where Advanced Marketing Seminars is run.

There is another "Basic Building Blocks to Success" seminar this weekend. Everybody's excited about it. Everybody assumes I'm going. I want to go, but it costs another $300, and it's in San Jose.

I'm frustrated. I'm sitting in the kitchen area doing nothing when Bill Gouldd walks in the front door of our office. I sit straight up and try to look busy. He walks by me. I'm about to breathe again when he turns around. "You're going this weekend, aren't you?"

"I want to."

"How does it feel to want?" He pauses. "I didn't ask if you want to; I asked if you are going."

"Well, my wife is pregnant and we spent all our money to get qualified, and then the desk rent and ads and my phone bill."

"Are you always that quick with excuses? You don't even give your mind one second to look for a solution before you stuff it with excuses."

I just look at him.

"If you can't afford to go, you can't afford not to."

"That's a nice little saying, but bottom line: I HAVE NO MONEY." I cannot even believe I've said it, and with an attitude, and to Mr. Gouldd, and in the office. I expect lasers to shoot from his eyes and turn me into the heap of smoking refuse I've become. But he's calm, almost friendly.

"Who is somebody you care a lot about?"

"My mom."

"Let's say you go home today and there is a message on your answering machine saying that your mom is deathly ill." I don't want to tell him I still live with my mom. "She has boils all over her body and a dangerously high temperature. Somehow she contracted a rare disease. She only has forty-eight hours to live. She's in a coma and you are the only one who knows. Only one doctor has the antidote and he just accepts cash—five thousand dollars. What do you do?" He draws me completely into the scenario. His eyes are an intense blue. I'm scared talking to him and scared for my mom.

"First I would go to Doug, my step-dad, then my grandparents and other family. I'd get the money!"

"So, you are willing to do anything to save your mom, but nothing to save yourself." He gets up and walks out.

It hits me hard. I'm being a wimp. Making excuses.

He walks back in. "Obviously, you're not going to die if you don't go this weekend. But, financially, you're drowning. I can teach you how to swim, but if you don't think your future is worth three hundred dollars, I don't either."

I am going. There is no doubt about it. I have no idea how, but I'm going.

I read in the book, *Think and Grow Rich,* about a general who uses a bold technique to conquer foreign countries. He sails to the distant land, unloads all of his troops on the beach, and orders the ships to be burned. He stands on the shore with the burning ships in the background and yells, "We win or we die!" They always win. They have no option.

I drive to San Jose with filters in my trunk. I only have enough money for gas up there, not back. I have no money for food, hotel, or the seminar. I have to sell the filters. I have no option.

I know no one in San Jose, so I figure I'll sell to restaurants. They need water filters.

"Excuse me, I need to speak with your manager."

"Can I ask what about?"

"It's a health-related issue." I figure this will get their attention.

"I'm the owner."

"Sir, my name is Rob Styler and I have the best water filter in the world for your restaurant. Your ice will be clearer, your drinks will taste better, the true flavor of your food will come out. Not only that, but you can write on your menus, 'All drinks, ice, and food in our restaurant are prepared with bottled-quality water because we care about your health.' People will feel a loyalty to your restaurant and will tell their friends. Your business will grow and you can have all this for two hundred and twenty dollars." I'm out of breath, but I didn't even stutter.

He laughs, "You seem excited."

"Oh, I am, sir. I drove up here from San Diego today with only these filters in my trunk. To even get back home, I have to sell them. But that's all going to change. This weekend I'm going to go to a seminar and learn about success from a multimillionaire. I just have to sell three filters to pay for the seminar, hotel, and food."

"Well, you definitely have the right attitude." He's starting to like me.

"Do you remember when you first started your restaurant?"

"Yes, that was twenty years ago."

"It is obvious that you're a success now, sir, but were there any times when you were getting started that one person helping you made the difference? One person lending a helping hand let you make the next step?"

He smiles. "There were many people." I look at him, expectantly asking him to go on. He smiles wider. "I'm not only going to buy your water filter, I'm going to buy you lunch." He turns and goes back to the kitchen.

Yes, yes, yes! I've done it, my first retail sale where I actually make money. I didn't even have to turn the water yellow.

We have a great conversation about what it took for him to get started, the hard times, the challenges. He does most of the talking. Before I leave, he gives me the addresses of two friends who own restaurants. He calls them and they both buy filters.

I make $660 in three hours because I've made a commitment. I've burned my bridges. I've made sure I have no option, no way out, and I've won. I think I could run faster than Pegasus.

The seminar is incredible. I can barely sit in my seat. I have an urge the whole weekend to stand on my chair and scream, "I did it!"

I drive home on fire. I'm going to be rich. No options, no excuses, just results.

I've already worked through the people I knew before the business, my "warm market." Most of my friends have written me off to temporary insanity. It's my fault. I treated them like I'd found the golden goose and they were still cleaning the stall. One friend put it well: "Rob, last week we all chipped in a buck so you could go to the movies with us. Now you're acting like you're the answer to our financial future. Just chill."

I tell Joe about this. He always has something to say that puts me back on track. "Same thing happened to me, man. A prophet is never welcome in his own hometown. My friends still saw me as who I had been. They couldn't break that mold and realize who I was becoming—so I bailed and found better friends. Bill Gouldd told me that if you want to know where you'll be in five years, just look at who you're hanging out with today. I freaked. I did not want to be like the surf bums I was hanging out with, so I bailed."

One childhood friend, Steve Abbey, says he'll help me. It means a lot. I have an ally. He drives down from Santa Barbara and brings a book on multilevel marketing. We make a plan. The guy who wrote the book says to use flyers. Makes sense to me. We print up a thousand flyers with Steve's money. I used to do graphic arts in college, so I make them look good. We print all the statistics about cancer, chemicals, and toxins. At the top in big letters, it reads, Are you poisoning your family?

We decide not simply to place these on cars or post them in laundromats. No, we roll each one and tie it with a red bow. We think that if we make the flyers look like a present or an invitation everybody will read them, realize their ignorance in poisoning their family, and immediately call us for the obvious solution. We stuff the rolled-up, hand-tied flyers in several Glad garbage bags and race around the neighborhood hooking the red bows over doorknobs.

We get back to my parent's home about 5 P.M., exhausted. But we have enough energy to get out the calculator and start projecting our incomes. We figure bare minimum we'll make $500 each. My parents promise that if we have the actual orders, paid for, they will order the product on their credit card so we can get it faster. Both Steve and I have cars, so we figure delivery to the homes won't be a problem. We're ready.

We wait for the phone calls. I figure they're just getting home. They're tired. They want to rest a bit before they call. Now they're eating dinner. They're not going to call at dinner. Now it's family time. They want to spend some quality time with the kids. Now they're probably putting the children to bed. They obviously want to wait until there are no distractions before they call. Their favorite TV show is probably on now. It's eight o'clock; all the best shows start at eight. By 11 P.M. I decide they're probably just too tired from their dead-end jobs and they're going to wait for the weekend. No one calls that weekend or any other weekend. Bill Gouldd had said, "Flyers don't work." I prove him right.

Steve wishes me luck, hops back in his truck, and heads back to Santa Barbara. Easy for him; he doesn't have $6,500 of his parents' money invested in this thing. I remember what I've been told repeatedly: "Your level of success is determined by your level of commitment." I don't know what more I can commit.

Then it happens. I'm looking out the window doing "the dealer walk." Dealers walk back and forth, looking out on the parking lot, watching for their ad calls to come. I'm a Car Qualified, but I still do it. A gray

Mercedes-Benz pulls up. The man is forty-five to fifty years old, distinguished, sharply dressed, wearing polished shoes. He walks with a confident stride. All of us claim him as our own. "He's going to ask for me. He's my pearl, baby." "No way, he's mine." We're like sharks that smell blood. This man incites a feeding frenzy.

"I'm here to meet Rob Styler." We're all in the kitchen as I hear this. I feel like I'm being crowned Miss America. Everybody looks at me. I'm supposed to smile, but I'm in shock. What am I supposed to say to this man? I cover my face with my hands and run back to the desk area, grabbing Marc along the way.

I talk fast: "Bud, you got to save me. This guy could make my business but I'm freaking. My heart is racing. Feel my pulse."

"Chill, dude. I'll talk to him, but you'll have to close him. I have to bail after the briefing. Don't make yourself the issue. It's the system, remember. Breathe, brother, breathe deep. You look like you're about to faint. Remember that he answered your ad. You've got the deal. Take control," Marc reassures me.

"Just talk to him, okay? Tell him . . . tell him I'll talk with him after the presentation. You're a life saver, dude." Spending this much time with Marc and Joe, I begin to talk like them.

I sit near the back of the room. I'm afraid if I sit next to him, he'll judge me, not the system. He's nodding. He's raising his hand. This is good. This is good.

Several of us have been trying our skills at doing part of the presentation. Today it's Mark Soda's turn. Soda's a nice guy and the man who I'd want on my basketball team. At 6'8", he has quite a presence, but when he gets nervous, he sweats. Doing the briefing, he's nervous. Rivulets of sweat are chasing down his face and dripping off his chin. My big chance, and he's sweating. He makes a mistake on the whiteboard and wipes the blue ink off with his left hand. He wipes the sweat from his forehead, and the blue ink smears the whole left side of his face. Blue sweat starts dripping off the end of his chin. The crowd is hysterical. I bury my face in the palms of my hands. He's making a few jokes and thinking he's on a roll, which makes the whole scene even funnier. It's a good briefing. People are excited because they had so much fun. After the briefing I have to talk with my guest.

"H . . . H . . . Hi, . . . I . . . I'm Rob Styler. Th . . . that was funny with the blue ink, huh?"

"I do not think I've been on an interview with as much laughter. It's a pleasure to meet you, Rob. I'm John Watkins. We spoke on the phone." His teeth are so white.

"So, what do you think?" I bite my tongue as I say this. At the last seminar, Bill Gouldd said never to say, "What do you think?" I am supposed to tell him what to think.

"I think this is incredible. I have a lot of friends who have made money in multilevel. I've passed up many opportunities where I would have made big money. But now the timing is right. I'm ready. I want to start with the five thousand dollars, and I have three friends I know will do the same. That will make me a Director, right?"

I stare at him, blinking. I don't say anything. It doesn't seem real. This is way too big for me to handle. Bill Gouldd taught me, "Fear is replaced by action." I spring to action. "Sheri, Sheri, I got one. I got one!" I race out of the room desperately searching for Sheri. She'll know what to do. I can't find her. I search each room. Nowhere.

I go back to the briefing room and he's gone. Gone! I rush to the window overlooking the parking lot and watch his gray Mercedes pull away.

Sheri later finds me and tries to comfort me. "Heard you lost a good one today."

"Yeah, I was so excited. I did everything wrong."

"Yeah, 'Sheri, I got one' probably isn't the best thing to yell through the office."

"I scared him away."

"He probably felt like a fish on hook." The visual makes me smile. "Call him back, Rob. Maybe he just got paged and had to rush off. I doubt it," she laughs, "but you never know. You'll find your pearl."

Our lives are shaped not as much by our experience
as by our expectations.

George Bernard Shaw

Chapter 8

If your compassion does not include yourself, it is incomplete.
The Buddha

The next big seminar is called "Journey Beyond Perception." Apparently, this one is less about business and more about life. We're going to learn universal success principles that will help us in all aspects of life. Marina and I have to go together because the training will bring our relationship to an unimaginable level of trust, understanding, and love. For both of us to go, I need to make some money.

I figure out a system to sell filters. It actually works. There's a Ralph's grocery store by my parents' house. I wait, patiently, watching the Aqua-Vend machine. Once they stick the quarter in to fill their jug, they can't leave. They have to talk to me. I pretend like I'm casually walking into Ralph's. I look at them as I'm walking by so they notice me, but then I continue. As soon as their guard is down, I turn, doing the "Columbo Close": "Excuse me, I don't mean to bother you, but I used to fill my jugs up all the time just like you're doing. It was such a hassle."

They answer, although most wonder why I'm telling them this. "Yeah, it's a hassle, but it's cheaper than bottled water and I won't drink from the tap." I can always tell by their body language. If they turn away from me, I walk away and wish them a nice day. If they turn toward me, I continue.

"You're a smart man not to drink the tap water," I pause. "A friend of mine showed me a filter that does the same thing as this big machine here but right on your sink, in your home. The best thing was, instead of costing thirty-five cents a gallon, it only cost two cents a gallon. I couldn't believe it until I tried it myself. He actually let me try it free for a few days." At this point their response varies, but I'm usually able to lead them in the direction I want. As Mr. Gouldd taught me, "It's a funny thing about knowing where you want to go; you usually get there."

I continue the pitch, "You know, I remember how much I used to hate filling those jugs. Why don't you let me call my friend and see if he'll let you try one of his systems free? It can't hurt. I can't guarantee he'll do it, but he is a friend." Now instead of being a salesman, I'm just a nice guy helping them out.

I would get their phone number and then call them that night. "Listen, my friend's way too busy selling these filters to come by your house, but he dropped off a filter with me and said I could let you try it." I sell seven filters. We get the money to go to "Journey."

People come from all over the country. It's like a reunion where I know only a small percentage of the family. Marina clings to me because she knows even fewer.

"Journey" begins as an adventure where we mentally travel back in time and discover how our positive and negative "programs" were first established. We discover how and why we "sabotage" our success. We do simple yet profound exercises which graphically demonstrate how our past programs influence our future. Each exercise is performed in groups of six people. We switch groups throughout the day.

The seminar lasts five days. On the last day, we design a blueprint of our future. We're supposed to write long-term and short-term goals for every aspect of our lives. I write a long-term goal for my house. *I enjoy the tranquillity, peace, and power I feel from purchasing my 3,000-square-foot, Santa Fe style home on five acres of land in November 1995.*

I'm not sure why I choose that date, but I get a surge of energy writing this goal. It's about three in the morning, we haven't slept in two days, and we haven't eaten in fourteen hours. We're all in a daze.

Mr. Gouldd's explaining the importance of writing our goals on light blue paper and using dark blue ink because the subconscious registers blue better than any color. Mr. Gouldd happens to be walking right by my table.

"Mr. Gouldd, I don't mean to bother you, but I have an idea."

He turns off his microphone and comes closer. "It's three o'clock. I haven't slept or eaten and you have an idea. What?" I can tell by his tone that I shouldn't have said anything. "Well, you've already disrupted my seminar, what is your all-important idea?"

"W . . . W . . . Well, I . . . I was just thinking about how you just said the subconscious mind absorbs blue better than any color."

"Yes, I just said that, and your point is . . . ?"

"I . . . I was just thinking that maybe next 'Journey' we could make the workbooks have light blue paper and dark blue ink so that our subconscious would absorb all of the information better." I say it all in one breath.

He turns his head to the side and speaks slowly. "You know, I've heard a lot of stupid ideas in my life. But I think you just won the fucking prize. That is the stupidest fucking idea I have ever heard in my life." He begins to walk toward the stage. He turns. The people at my table lean away from me. "And, oh, by the way, don't even worry about the next 'Journey' because you're too fucking stupid to even be here next time."

I stare without blinking as he turns his microphone back on and walks back to the stage. First the baseball incident and now this. Maybe I am stupid. All the people at my table avoid eye contact with me.

Before "Journey," this incident would've crushed me. But I've learned a lot these past five days. I've learned to listen and understand another person's perspective before reacting. Instead of getting angry or defensive or crushed, I take three deep breaths and reread two quotations from the seminar: "We would lead happier, more successful lives if we simply acted on the advice we give to others," and "We best teach what we most need to learn."

I've learned it's not what happens, but how I choose to respond to what happens that matters. I decide I *will* be back next "Journey." I decide to prove him wrong. I decide to make it a motivator rather than a de-motivator. I still feel stupid, but not as powerless.

Overall, it's an amazing five days. I cry. I laugh. I grow. I change. My favorite color is no longer blue.

This is my fourth month in the business. Not one person has signed up in my organization. Everybody keeps telling me how great I'm doing. I raise my hand all the time in the briefing. I've got my fake laugh down to an art. I'm positive. Whenever somebody asks how I'm doing, I say, "Unbelievable!" And it is. I have nobody, zero, zilch, *nada*, in my sales force. That's unbelievable.

After the briefing, I expect people not to sign up. Nobody else has; why should they? My business becomes a self-fulfilling prophecy. I have a twisted, deep-seated program that actually hopes they won't sign up. It's okay for me to try something and fail. It's not okay for me to bring someone else into the business and have them fail because they followed me. How can I sign someone up when I've made no money? My simple solution is, I don't.

Every week we have a national conference call with Mr. Gouldd during which he shares exciting, motivational stories of people across the country. "Suzy, you've been working out in Dallas for two months. I hear you just made Director and got a check for over eight thousand dollars. How does it feel?"

"Oh, Mr. Gouldd, it's just incredible. I've never done anything like this before, but the system makes it so simple. All I do is bring my people to the seminars. I could not believe it when I got my check. I had no idea it was going to be that big."

"That's great, Suzy, congratulations. Victor in Chicago, are you there?"

"Yes, sir, Mr. Gouldd."

"I heard you retailed twelve thousand dollars worth of product your first month. Is that true?"

"Yes, sir, these products sell themselves." I begin to wonder if I'm living in the wrong city.

"And how much was your net profit?"

"I made over six thousand dollars my first month, sir."

"That's a little more than you make as a teacher, right?"

"Considerably more, sir."

I keep waiting for him to call out, "Rob in San Diego! I understand you've been full time in the business for four months, and not one person has signed up in your sales force. I also heard you actually lost money on your first retail sale. How does it feel?" LOSER. That's what it feels like. But it actually makes me more resolved not to quit.

Winners never quit, and quitters never win is taped on the inside of my briefcase. If these other people are getting rich, I can, too. My learning curve is just flatter at the beginning. But wait till I catch momentum. "The race is not always to the swift, but to those who keep running." I like this one because I ran cross-country and track in college. We had another saying, "When the going gets tough, the sprinters stop." That's all these instant success stories are: they're sprinters. I'm pacing myself for long-term success.

One of my current favorite sayings is, "If you are walking through hell, don't stop."

Everybody keeps telling me, "You're just building stories, man. When you're a millionaire, you'll be able to relate to the new people because of what you're going through now." I have plenty of stories. I would like to start building income.

I still have the one suit that Mom bought me on sale at Men's Wearhouse for $179. I remember thinking, "How do they expect me to get rich if I have to spend all this money on clothes?" I wear it every day. I only have one tie, but Steve Baran, Joe Locke, and I have a system. Steve has one tie, I have one tie, and Joe has two. We swap. The new people only come in a few times a week, so they don't catch on, and the associates would never say anything. That would be bringing neg energy into the office.

I begin to notice inconsistencies in the office, but I never mention anything. I get to the office extra early one morning, and Joe and Marc are showering in the downstairs bathroom. They say the plumbing is out in their apartment, but from the look of their car, that is their apartment.

I've taken over the desk and phone line of Lori Rubidge, one of the top people. I keep getting phone calls for her saying it is very important that she return their calls. They leave 800-numbers. I'm getting the same calls at home from bill collectors. But Lori Rubidge is a Knight of the Round Table. She has to be a millionaire. She couldn't be getting calls from bill collectors.

I tell Sheri about the calls. She looks at the list. "I'll take care of it, Rob. Thanks."

The next day I get a call from Lori, who is actually more motivated than Casey. She's extremely friendly and positive, but as we hang up the phone I feel like I did something wrong. She makes it clear that any other messages should be forwarded directly to her. I should never bother Ms. Sharman.

At the office, I'm excited. At home, the bills and the pressure keep mounting. I have no money to pay my bills, but I feel a perverse obligation to open and read each one. "Can't pay this one. Can't pay this one either. Oh, they're getting mad." I do this twisted ritual before I try to sleep. Not a good idea. Instead of getting the rest I desperately need, I stare at the ceiling, thinking they will probably repossess my child when he's born.

Not only do I read each bill, but I also place each one on the refrigerator with magnets. Somehow I think this makes me responsible. The bills don't get paid. But I induce insomnia and indigestion.

My life is one continuous roller coaster. Excited at the office. Depressed at home. Excited at the office. Depressed at home. I begin to spend every waking hour at the office.

One day, a Thursday, things change. "How many bills did we get today?" I ask Marina. This is often my first question when I get home.

"None."

"None?"

"Not one bill." I check the calendar. It's not a national holiday.

"Was the mail delivered today?"

"Your parents got stuff." Twenty-six years old, married, and I'm still living with my parents.

"That's weird, no bills." Confused, I go to sleep.

Next day, same thing. Saturday, no bills. It's been over a week now, and we have not received one bill in the mail. I'm starting to get excited. Maybe they forgot—computer error. It happens. I've seen movies like *It's a Wonderful Life*. Miracles happen. Maybe they all got together and said, "This guy is pathetic. We're just wasting our letters and phone calls. Let's make him our yearly charity case." I feel like I've won the lottery.

The next day Sheri calls me into her office. "Rob, you have been working hard. I'm proud of you. You're going to make a lot of money in this company. I'm counting on you to be one of my top leaders. We have to work on your image, though. I want you in front of the room. I want you to do the briefings and trainings. But you need a new suit."

"I know, Sheri. Believe me, I know." I've worn the same suit every day for three months. Every Wednesday I go to the same dry cleaner and sit in a back room reading a book in my underwear while they dry-clean my suit in less than an hour. The owners think it's funny. I try to laugh.

"I know things are tight for you financially right now, Rob. You're paying your dues. But you have the right attitude." She pulls out a large business checkbook. I stop looking at her eyes and stare at the checkbook. She continues, "I'm going to loan you five hundred dollars. Go out and get a nice, dark, double-breasted suit, two shirts, three ties, and a nice pair of shoes." She writes the check. I take it without words. Tears well up in my eyes. I stare at her.

"Don't say anything, Rob. I'm betting on you."

Sheri Sharman believes in me. She's betting on me. I remember when Sam Adams bet on me. He was the head track coach at the University of California at Santa Barbara (UCSB). I was the only person on the team to qualify for the NCAA Cross-Country Western Regional Championships. I was proud but alone. I had to fly up alone. Race alone. It didn't feel the same without the team. I was coming down a hill with about two miles to go, and there was Coach, cheering me on. He was there, all on his own, for me. I was exhausted but I got a second wind and passed six people. I still only placed forty-second. But when I think of that race, I rarely think of where I placed; I just remember he was there for me.

I have a new attitude. Sheri's betting on me and I have a new suit, new shirts, new ties, and new shoes. I feel good. I feel great! I'm excited and my business reflects it. People not only say they're going to come back the next day—they actually come back.

My enthusiasm is contagious. Two people sign up and pay their $20 for the application. But they never come back. I call repeatedly, but they don't return my messages. Over a week goes by, and I ask Joe for advice.

"Joe, I had two people come in last week, fill out their applications, pay for them, and now they won't return my phone calls. Have you ever had that happen?"

"Where are the applications?"

"Here."

Joe walks over, takes the applications and tears off the twenty-dollar bills I'd stapled to them. He hands me the money. "Lunch money."

"What?"

"Lunch money. Rob, some people are going to be with you when you reach the top of the mountain. Others help you get there. These kind of people feed you along the way." I look at him half smiling, half confused. I'm happy that I have $40 in my hand, but I thought I was supposed to send it to the company.

Joe continues, "They just gave you the twenty dollars to get out of here. They're so spineless they couldn't even tell you they weren't interested. They will never do anything, whether you send in that application or not. Wait a few weeks if it makes you feel better. If they start to work, send in their application. If not, eat well, my skinny friend. Who deserves that money more, the paper pushers at NSA, or you?" I'm beginning to see his point. My first application payments are converted into several all-I-can-eat meals at the Souplantation.

I get home late again. I go to the outside garbage can to throw away an apple core. I stare in disbelief. The bills are in the trash. I grab the letters and march into the house.

"Marina, did you throw these bill away?"

She looks like a child caught cheating. "Yes."

"Why?" I'm trying to stay calm.

"Because every time you read the bills you get upset, so I throw them away," she says quickly.

I have to smile. Marina doesn't understand bills. She comes from a little village in Guatemala. There, they don't receive bills, because they have no services for which to be billed. I remember when we first came to the States. After a few times of using my ATM card, Marina asked, "When am I going to get my free money card?" Much of my culture does not make sense to her.

What she understands is that bills bring stress. Get rid of bills; get rid of stress. It works. Even after knowing she's been throwing the bills away, I'm still able to keep my positive attitude. The situation hasn't changed, but my attitude has.

This month is a turning point in my business. When I first started four months ago, I wrote a letter to the most financially successful person I knew. He finally responds:

"Rob, I know little about multilevel marketing, but I know people and I know business. That Bill Gouldd knows his business. Treat it like an education. You will learn more in two years working with him than you could in any graduate school in the country. He has street smarts. He knows how to motivate and manipulate human beings.

"Just be careful, because he is a smart man. He makes money whether you do or not. While you're out there pounding the pavement, he is at home making money. When you buy product, he makes money. When you go to his seminars, he makes money. When you buy his tapes or other material, he makes money. He has created a money machine. There is nothing wrong with that. But if you decide to be part of it, just make sure you get a piece of it."

Sound advice. I hear only the first part—I am getting a top graduate school education. Life is good.

I'm eating my bag lunch on the porch outside the office, one of the rare times I'm actually away from my phone. I come back to my desk and the answering machine is blinking. No calls all day, I leave for fifteen minutes and, *bang*, a message that's destined to alter my financial future.

It's from Armando T. Perez from Tijuana. I've been running an ad for people who are bilingual. I hesitate calling him back. It's an international call. It'll cost at least a dollar. Finally, I do it anyway.

"Hello, my name is Rob Styler, and I'm calling for Armando Perez."

"*Qué?*" At times I speak so quickly people can't understand me. This time it must be a language barrier. I am calling Mexico.

"*Lla . . . Lla . . . Lla . . . Llamo por Armando Perez.*" Damn stutter.

I hear in the background, "Armando, some gringo calling for you."

"Ask him what he wants."

"What do you want?"

"Armando called me about an advertisement for people who are bilingual."

"Mando, it's about a job, man."

"Tell him I changed my mind, I got a job."

"He changed his mind. He got a job."

"I heard." By this time, I'm calculating how much this is going to cost me on next month's phone bill.

"My name is Rafael Rojas. I'm bilingual, man. I speak Spanish and English. What's the job?"

He sounds enthusiastic. I heard the first minute of the call costs the most anyway.

"We're an international marketing firm that focuses on environmental solutions."

"I like marketing, man. I do some work with a marketing company. I help load the trucks."

"That sounds great. What I would like to do is set up an interview where I can give you all of the necessary information and can also learn more about your experiences and ambitions. That sounds fair, doesn't it?"

"Yeah, that sounds great. When?"

"How is Saturday morning at ten o'clock for you?"

"*Está bien.*"

"What's your name again?"

"Rafael Rojas."

Rafael's coming Saturday. I've always wanted to work the Spanish-speaking market. I have a good feeling about this. There's another "Basics" this weekend, but I'm selected to stay and keep the office open. I think Sheri knows I have no money for the seminar. There are only three of us left to run the office. I have to do the briefing. This will be my first time doing the whole presentation. I have done short parts, but never the whole thing.

Rafael comes early, the only person to show up. His hair is slicked back on the sides, curly and below his shoulders in the back. He's wearing a shiny, light blue silk suit that looks like one the bullfighters wear. The jacket is cropped short at the waist, and his shirt is ruffled and open at the chest. He's skinnier than I am. There are six small round mirrors down the outside of his pants. It's obvious he's put much thought and preparation into his appearance. It's not obvious that he will change my life.

It's time for the briefing. I'm nervous, but I've seen it every day, twice a day, for the past four months. I begin from memory.

"Hi, my name is Rob Styler. I'm sure most of you are more accustomed to a one-on-one interview. As you can see, from the way we're growing, that would be impossible." Until Rafael begins to look around the room, it doesn't dawn on me that he's the only new person here. He knows it. I feel stupid and start to stutter. I hate that stuttering. I stammer my way through the first part of the briefing and put the video in.

I go into the kitchen and take deep, relaxing breaths. The second part of the briefing goes more smoothly. Rafael is fairly disinterested until the testimonials. I put in the testimonial video, go outside the room, and watch him through the slightly ajar door. As soon as the people on the video mention how much money they've made, Rafael leans forward. The more money they quote, the more he leans forward. Lan Tran, a small Vietnamese fireball of a lady, comes on screen.

"Hi, I Lan Tran. I no sure what I do, but I get check for ten thousand dollars. Ten thousand dollars! I no believe it, but bank say yes. This American Dream."

I turn on the lights, pop out the video, and begin to close the briefing.

Rafael interrupts me, "You don't need to say anything else, man. Just tell me what I have to do and let me talk to Lan Tran." Rafael had met Lan when he first came in. Now they talk for twenty minutes. Rafael fills out his application, gives me his last twenty dollars, and promises to return at 10 A.M. on Monday with his roommate, Armando, the person who originally answered the ad. Rafael signs up in spite of me.

On Monday morning, they both come back. Armando has a much heavier build and is wearing a white shirt/jacket, open to the navel with kung-fu figures decorating the lapel. Rafael has another bullfighter suit, different color. They're quite a sight, and they're excited. I explain about buying product at wholesale, starting their own business, being capitalists. They decide to start with the $500 line of credit. I try to contain my excitement.

Rafael has no money, so he borrows it from Armando. They have been best friends since grammar school.

Rafael buys six filters on the credit line. The next day they come back.

"Okay. Now I'm going to teach you how to sell the filters you bought yesterday." This should be interesting. I'm going to teach them what I can't do myself.

They both look at each other. Rafael says, "We did that yesterday. Is that okay, man?"

"Y . . . Y . . . Yeah, that's great." They sold them yesterday! I try to stay calm. "Did you sell them all?"

"Yeah, it was easy."

"And the people paid retail, two hundred and twenty dollars each?"

84

They both laugh. "Actually they paid a little more. I hope that's all right."

"Yeah, it's great!" I'm in shock. But, remembering the "Sheri, I got one" incident, I try not to show it. They have sold more filters in one day than I have in four months. I've found my pearls.

Next weekend there's a "Basics" in Los Angeles. They have to go. I have to convince them.

"Rafael, Armando, you know about the 'Basics' this weekend, right?"

"Yeah, we know," Rafael responds.

"You're going, right? This will be the best possible thing you could do for your future. If you learn the information directly from Bill Gouldd, in five years you could retire."

"That's great. But right now, for both of us, it would cost six hundred dollars. We don't have six hundred dollars."

"What do you mean? You just sold all your filters last weekend. You should have an extra one thousand dollars."

"That was last weekend. Do you know how long it's been since we've had cash in our pockets? This weekend we went to Baby Rock Disco. Tequila. Champagne. *Mujeres*. No more money."

"We have no money. *Nada*," shares Armando.

"You spent a thousand dollars in one night at a disco?" I say in disbelief.

"But it was a good night," Armando laughs.

Rafael philosophizes, "You either get busy living, or get busy dying. I saw that in a movie once. And we were living Saturday night, right Armando?!"

"Living large!"

I could live for two months on that money. I excuse myself to the bathroom, my refuge. *They spent a thousand dollars in one night.*

I get back and they're both speaking with Casey. They are excited. She's telling them how beautiful the women will be at the seminar. Why didn't I think of that? Here are two people who obviously live for the moment, and I'm trying to sell them on the future. Thank God for Casey.

They decide only one can go, and they can afford only $300 for everything.

"No problem," I say. "You pay for the seminar and I'll take care of the transportation, food, and lodging."

"You got a deal, gringo."

I did it. Rafael is going to the seminar.

I think his idea of "transportation, food, and lodging" is different from mine. He is not excited about Pegasus. I had learned earlier not to introduce people who were interested in the business to Pegasus. My prospects would walk excitedly down to the parking lot to get a brochure or a product. As soon as they could tell which car I was heading toward, they would stop ten feet from Pegasus and ask, "This is your car?"

"Yes, I call it Pegasus."

"You know, I want to think about this business a little more. This is a big decision. I'll get back to you." They never would. Another lesson on image.

Rafael doesn't have a choice. He has already prepaid for his seminar, but I can see the fear in his eyes as we merge with the freeway. Besides the loose door, Pegasus has a bent frame. (An earlier accident has made the frame angle off the road.) She drives straight, but the sensation can be disconcerting until you're used to it. Marina is in the back. Rafael is quiet. His knuckles are white on the door handle. I think he's concerned about both his safety and his decision. Pegasus is the first tangible evidence he's had that I'm not doing well, and he's just invested $300 of his best friend's money to follow my lead.

All three of us go to the Friday night briefing. Bill Gouldd's amazing. Rafael's ecstatic. The Man does his magic. It's working; just get them to see the Big Guy.

Rafael seems to be used to the car now, but the lodging is a shock. I think he thought I meant a hotel. Hotels cost money. I have something different in mind. Marina's brother Oscar has a house in the mountains. He is the caretaker for Santiago Lake in Orange County. As we drive farther into the mountains, Rafael looks worried. He doesn't know me, and we keep driving farther and farther up a twisting, deserted road. I pull left into a side street and stop in front of an old locked gate. The key is beneath a rock at the base of the metal post. No Trespassing signs are everywhere.

"Where are we?" Rafael finally asks, trying to sound calm.

"This is where we're sleeping."

"I'm no Boy Scout. I want a bed."

"Of course, only the finest homey accommodations for my new friend. Hotels are stuffy. Here we get to breathe fresh, crisp, mountain air. Our minds will be clear for what we'll learn tomorrow."

"I just hope I don't get eaten by coyotes. I have a cousin in Durango who got attacked by a whole pack of them. They tore him to bits. Dead."

"Don't worry, Rafael, you'll be protected by four solid walls." Little does he know they'll be the four sides of a VW bus.

So far transportation has been Pegasus, lodging is a bus, and in the morning Rafael finds out food is two days of peanut butter and jelly sandwiches. He's not a happy camper.

But as he walks into the seminar, everybody's dancing, the music is loud, and the smell of burning sage drifts from the back of the room. It smells like marijuana. Rafael, who has barely spoken to me all morning, looks at me with excitement, "They're smoking the herb, what a company!" He works his way to the front of the room, jumps up on the first row of chairs, and starts dancing—and I mean *dancing*. The boy can move. People start cheering. He's in his element. I smile, knowing that last night, sleeping in the bus, is the last thing on his mind.

> *Triumph: umph added to try.*
> Theodore Roosevelt

Chapter 9

And if the blind lead the blind, both shall fall into a pit.
Matthew 15:14

"Bill Gouldd is the answer. My whole life I've been looking, and now I've found the answer." Rafael is excited. I'm excited. Rafael is in my sales force.

We get back to San Diego, and he and Armando go to work. They start talking to everyone. They bring their friends from the restaurant where they used to work. They bring co-workers from the loading dock. They drag down friends of friends. Most are interested, but they won't buy anything.

Rafael begins to get frustrated. "We've brought all of these people down and not one person has signed up and bought product." I've learned that my job as a "leader" is to get them to stop focusing on the problem. I need to direct them down the path I want them to follow and demonstrate that I have the answer for them.

"Rafael, the reason your people haven't committed is you haven't committed. They are waiting for you to set the pace, to lead them. How can you expect someone to follow what you haven't done?"

"I'm committed. I bought product and went to a seminar," he says defensively.

"That's like opening a restaurant, buying food for one day's meals, taking one cooking class, and saying, 'I tried.' You have to keep reinvesting in your business. You made a profit your first day, and then you spent it all on women and alcohol."

"So? It was my money."

"And it's your business, too. What you do with it depends on what you put into it. You were committed those first days. You bought product, sold product, and now your business is stagnant. If you want people to follow in your footsteps, you have to move your feet. You're a Dealer trying to get other Dealers to make a commitment. You need to become a Manager and watch what happens."

"I don't have the money."

"You need to find the money." I walk away.

I can't believe it. I want to do a jig. Bill Gouldd's words came out of my mouth. He would've done way better, of course, but I used analogies, I made valid points, and then I walked away closing him with fear of loss. Yes, that was powerful.

But, what if he gets pissed off and leaves? What if he decides he can't do it? What if he quits and I lose the only real person in my sales force? I go back to the kitchen area where we have just spoken. He's gone, my first and only good person, gone. Me, trying to play Bill Gouldd. What a joke.

Fortunately, my desk is the last one in the row at the back of the office. Whenever I'm feeling like this I put my briefcase on the desk, open it up ninety degrees, hide behind the leather, and reread *Think and Grow Rich*.

The next day Rafael comes back with the money. He walks in the office and says, "I got it." Again, I try not to act surprised. But my face gives me away.

"You're surprised, right?" he says with a confident grin.

"No, I knew you'd do it."

"Liar." I've never been a good liar. "You thought I'd never come back. Oh, ye of little faith. I'm going to make you so much money." That statement turns out to be prophetic.

Rafael convinced Armando to sell his motorcycle. They got $4,500. The problem is that they both want to become Managers and they both need enough money to go to the "Leadership" seminar, which is in New Jersey. The seminar costs $495 each, and then there's the flights and food. I offer to take care of the lodging.

"But we're going to stay in a hotel, right?" Rafael says with a smile. They constantly tease me about that first night in the "convee." Each time he tells the story, the coyotes get closer, and the sandwiches are staler.

We make a deal. This is something I learned from Marc. Once you are Director or above in the marketing plan, you can "qualify" anyone for any position before Director—for nothing if you want. I'm not a Director, but Marc gave me the inside scoop. The trick is to get as much money as possible because the more money we send to NSA, the bigger the checks we get. To quote Bill Gouldd, "Don't whore out the marketing plan. If you give away Manager for a thousand dollars, the position has no value for them. It's a five-thousand-dollar position. Make them earn it." But as I look over at Rafael and Armando I think, *They're trying so hard.* Naturally, I'm a wimp again.

"Tell you what I'll do. If you both go to the "Leadership" seminar and invest three thousand dollars in product, I'll make you both Managers." They look at each other like they've just found hidden cookies.

"Deal," they say in unison.

To afford the trip and the seminar, I have to sell a silver bar given to me when my father died, my only inheritance. It doesn't bother me at all. From what I hear, this seminar is the one thing I'm missing. I've got the basics; I understand interpersonal skills and relationships; now I'm going to learn to be a leader.

I get to the hotel at 6 P.M. Rafael and Armando are supposed to arrive at about 7 P.M. I figure I'll wait for them for dinner, so I watch some TV. It's the first TV I've watched in months, because I've been told, "There's no PV in TV." PV is personal volume.

Bill Gouldd says not to watch the news. Don't read the newspaper. When you have the financial resources to do something about what is happening in the world, learn about it. Until then, just stay focused on building your business. The news is designed to keep us scared, powerless, and controllable. The media creates fear to separate and manipulate us. If you want to get rich, you have to control what goes in your brain twenty-four hours a day. Don't listen to the radio; listen to educational cassette programs. Don't read the newspaper; read positive motivational books. Don't watch television; call a prospect.

As I watch TV, my fear grows. They aren't coming. They've spent the money at some bar in Tijuana. It's 10 P.M. They aren't coming. I leave several messages on Rafael's pager with the number of the hotel room, asking them to please call me. Finally, at 1 A.M., fatigue and jet lag create a restless sleep.

BANG, BANG, BANG! BANG, BANG, BANG! *What, what is that, who?* I stumble to the door. Rafael and Armando are standing in the hall. I'm half-awake but happy to see them. It's obviously raining outside. They look like wet rats.

"What happened to you guys? Where have you been?"

"Don't ask, Rob. It was a disaster." Rafael looks dazed.

"A nightmare," says Armando.

"You two look like you just lost your dog." They both half-smile, looking down at the ground.

"Rob, you would not believe what happened." My concern turns to curiosity.

"What? Tell me."

"Shit, man," Rafael begins. "First, we fly into the wrong airport. We have to take a shuttle and a taxi. We're spending money way too fast and we're pissed at you for not being more specific about the airport. We've never been east of Dallas.

"There's a bar at the airport and we need tequila. Two women start eyeing us. I like women." As he says this, his face contorts into a sly grin.

"They start flirting with us. I mean they're really coming on to us. We buy them a drink. Then the cute one puts her hand on my thigh and says we should get a hotel room. What were we supposed to do, say, 'No, we can't, our sponsor is expecting us?' We were pissed at you about the airport anyway.

"We buy a bottle of tequila and find a cheap hotel. We figure, *How often does something like this happen?* Like you always tell us, we were building stories." They both laugh.

"So we get real drunk. We fool around a little bit, but they were just teases. Mando and I both fall asleep and the bitches steal our pants and the rest of the money we had. They took everything. We're fucked."

"No way, they stole your money!"

"And our fucking pants. They were my mirrored ones, too. Those were some nice pants."

"How did you get here from the hotel?"

"We met some Mexican dude who felt sorry for us," Rafael says with a sigh.

"Fuck, Rob, we just want to sleep. Can we talk in the morning?" Armando looks like he's about to collapse. They fall asleep. I know I should feel sorry for them, but I don't. Picturing them waking up from a drunken stupor and finding their pants gone makes me giggle. I try to laugh quietly.

Of course, I have to pay for everything all weekend. I begin to wonder if the story wasn't a little too incredible and convenient. Rafael and Armando are hung over and get little out of Saturday. Now I'm pissed.

"You guys spend all your money to come out here this weekend, and then you get drunk, chase a couple of women, and get robbed. It serves you right. We have a chance to change our futures, to learn directly from a multimillionaire, and all you guys can think of is women and getting drunk. If you can be pulled off-track so easily, you'll never get rich." I sound like I'm speaking from a position of wealth.

They're quiet Saturday night. Sunday, they're on fire. Both of them are standing on the front row of chairs, leading the crowd in dance. I'm in awe of how confident they are. I position myself toward the middle of a group and wiggle my butt just enough so I don't stand out, but I'm dancing.

Bill Gouldd is in rare form. "We are going to create the most powerful, cohesive, marketing machine in history. We will take any product and be able to create worldwide distribution in twenty-four hours. The sales force will already be in place. We will just plug in the products. Some of you in this room will be opening up other countries, other continents.

"Some of you will not even be part of it. You will find some weak reason to quit and for the rest of your life you'll have to live with the fact that you were in the right place at the right time but didn't have what it takes to make it. You couldn't cut it. What's it going to be? What excuse are you going to come up with? What is going to be a good enough reason for you to miss out on the greatest opportunity of your life?

"We'll do this seminar again next year, and half of you won't be here. Why? Your obstacles will become bigger than your vision. Right now your vision is huge, because you're feeding off my vision. Because of the energy being created in this room, most of you are experiencing a larger, more vivid view of life than you've ever experienced. You're excited. But it's an artificial environment we've created. It's easy here. The hard part comes when you go home. When your wife asks you, 'Making any money yet?' When your co-workers laugh at you. When you question yourself. That's the trick. Not what others say to you, but what you say to yourself.

"What does that quiet little voice inside of you whisper? Does it hold you back or push you forward? It used to tell me I couldn't do it. It used to tell me, why even try? You've been a loser your whole life. But one day I took control. I visualized taking that little voice by the ankles and smashing his skull against a brick wall. I saw the whole thing. The skull splitting open, the brains splatting against the bricks. The little voice got quieter. And when he spoke, he was more respectful. Sometimes he would go back to his old ways. I had many techniques. Sometimes it was a forty-five to the forehead. BANG! The whole back of his head, splattered across a white wall. He began to learn. I trained him. I took control of that little voice." He pauses. "Who controls your voice? Who controls your subconscious? Is it your mom, your dad, your third-grade schoolteacher who said you weren't smart enough, you weren't good enough? I'm here to tell you, you are smart enough. You are good enough. Ninety-five percent of you have way more talent than I did when I started this journey.

"I know some of you think I came out of the womb with a double-breasted suit and a Rolex. Let me show you a video clip that will give you some perspective. Guys, run the video."

Bill Gouldd, 1984, shows on the screen.

It can't be him. It looks and sounds like a twin brother who never matured. He's goofy. His suit doesn't fit. His haircut is shaggy. He's skinny. If he's changed that much in six years, there's a chance for me.

When we get back to San Diego, Rafael and Armando start cranking. They no longer ask people, they tell them. *You are signing up. You are buying product. You are bringing your friends tomorrow.* It works. Like Bill Gouldd said, "People are desperately waiting to be led."

Each day their group gets bigger. More people bring more people. It's amazing to see the business working the way it is supposed to. I ask Sheri what I should do, how I should help Rafael. She responds with a smile, "Just stay out of his way." This becomes my managing philosophy with Rafael. He's better than I am at the business, so the less I "help," the better.

By the end of the month, he has about thirty people interested. Twenty are doing a courtesy credit plan. He does over $20,000 in volume, all with courtesy credit plans, all with small orders, and becomes a Director. The policy is if you do $20,000 in one "leg," you have to do at least $10,000 in your other "legs" to become a Director. You can't just "ride" the volume. Fortunately, with Rafael's success, my results also begin to improve. I develop another leg by telling ad calls that, because of Rafael's success, I have "excess volume" to help them get qualified. Three people do $2,000 orders and one does $1,000. I make all four of them Managers.

I'm desperate. I have to become a Director this month. I can't have Rafael a Director and me a Car Qualified. I end up with over $27,000 in volume in my organization. Sheri pulls some strings and gets me Director. Not only am I a Director, but I have a Director in my group and momentum. I'm going to be another Lori Rubidge.

Lori has been my patron saint since I started the business. Not only did I inherit her old desk, but also her story keeps me going whenever the thought of quitting creeps into my mind. I remember the first time I heard Lori's story. It was my first week in the business. She had made a conference call from Chicago: "I went four months without one person in my sales force. Why? Because I was trying to do it my way. The way I learned in college. I was a marketing major. Why did I need to go to a sales seminar? First, the seminars cost money I didn't have, and second, I thought if I was working for the company, they should pay me to be trained. Isn't that the way it's supposed to work? Yeah, if you want to be an employee with no future. Finally, Gary Henk, my sponsor, got me to go to a seminar. Wow. Everything clicked. More important, I got my people to go to their first seminar.

"They were even more excited than I was. We went to work. I got a check for twenty-four thousand dollars." She paused for effect. I was affected. "Think if I would have quit that fourth month. I'd be one of those people calling your ads saying, 'I tried one of these things and they don't work!' " She paused. Then with even more enthusiasm, "This does work! You just have to go to a seminar and learn how to make it work. Remember, there are only three rules: *Get excited, pay attention, and never, ever, ever quit!*"

That conference call becomes my inspiration. It keeps me going. *What if this is the month I make $24,000? I have to keep going.* That fifth month, my check is not as big as Lori's, but I make almost $5,000. I have momentum. I have Rafael.

*Nothing you do or think or wish or make is necessary
to establish your worth.*
From A Course in Miracles

Rafael Rojas.

Chapter 10

*We cannot teach people anything; we can only help them
discover it within themselves.*

Galileo Galilei

Business is booming now. Everybody's talking about my check. I'm working my way up the ranks of the office. One day Sheri tells me it is time to do the first Spanish briefing. I'm excited and scared. Then I remember Sheri doesn't speak Spanish. As long as I'm animated, she'll think I'm doing great. I could be selling Herbalife and she wouldn't know it.

We invite everyone; we're working like crazy. The first-ever Spanish briefing. We have the chairs set up. I'm going to do the first part and Rafael will do the close. We have it all planned.

Nobody comes. It's just Rafael, Armando, and me. Sheri's going to be here in five minutes to witness the big event. I'm panicking. I grab three Spanish-speaking people who clean the office: "How would you like to work in this office instead of clean it?" I'm not sure if they understand what I'm talking about, but they take a seat in the briefing room. The first Spanish briefing has lined up in the front row—Rafael, the three cleaning people, and Armando.

To Sheri's credit, she is just as excited and animated as if there are a hundred people in the room. Every time I say *agua* or *dinero* she yells excitedly, "I know that word!" It's a beginning.

One month later Sheri tells me it's time for me to go. I have to leave the office.

"What did I do wrong, Sheri?"

"Nothing, Rob," she laughs. "We just need an office closer to Mexico. You've been in this office too long. You're ready to open your own office. It's time. You're ready."

I don't feel ready. They're kicking me out of the nest, my cocoon. I'm off-balance all day. In the afternoon we have an association meeting.

We sit nervously in our chairs. We can feel it. Sheri's pissed.

She begins emotionally. "This is my home, my life. These sculptures on the shelves are from my living room. I want to make this place warm, like a home." She pauses. Her voice starts to crack. "How do you think it makes me feel when I see trash in the kitchen? When I see plants dying from no water? When I see spots on the carpet? Are all of you too good to clean?" Her anger mounts. "Are all you big money earners too professional to get your hands dirty? I used to scrub this office every night. Every night! This is your business. Your mom doesn't work here. Keep it clean! Am I understood?"

"Yes, Sheri. We're sorry." "Sorry, Sheri." "It won't happen again." "We'll keep it clean, sorry." We feel like punished children.

Sheri continues, "You guys need to step up. Be responsible. You've all been sucking off my energy for too long. Rob's stepping up. He's going out and opening his own office." Everybody claps. "How does it feel to be a leader, Rob?"

"Scary." Wrong answer.

"Scary? I personally pick you to open the second office in San Diego and you're scared. Maybe I need to reevaluate my choice." She looks straight at me as she pauses. "*Exciting* would be a better word. Don't you think, Rob?"

"Yes." I feel like I just peed on the carpet.

The next day I'm driving down to Chula Vista to find the office. I have certain guidelines: easy to locate, plenty of parking, 24-hour air conditioning, 24-hour access, 1,500 to 3,000 square feet, and a flexible landlord. This last one is of prime importance since I have no credit and no money.

Marina is now eight months pregnant, I have not made much money yet, and I am looking to sign a lease that obligates me to pay over $100,000 dollars over the next three years. I keep trying to remember why Sheri said I should be excited.

I find a great place in the middle of downtown Chula Vista, right next to the movie theaters. Everybody knows where the movie theaters are. Plenty of parking. Twenty-four hour access and air conditioning. Perfect. We negotiate the lease. Actually, the owner tells me what he wants me to pay, and I say okay.

"All I have is five thousand dollars left from my last check," I plead with the owner.

"Well, normally we would need a much larger deposit." He pauses, scratching the back of his head. "Tell you what I'll do. Give me five thousand dollars for the first month's rent and deposit. As long as you agree to the twenty-four-hundred-dollar-a-month lease payment and sign the lease agreement, we'll let you move into the office in two weeks." I notice most of the other offices in the complex are empty. We move in August 13, 1990.

Kelby Morgan Styler is born August 31, 1990. We use a midwife instead of going to the hospital. Marina is petite, only 4'11", so there is some concern about her size. The midwife's birthing room is set up like a bedroom: thick comforters and carpets, hand-made quilts, beautiful pictures, soft light. Doug and Mom are there. Marina waddles back and forth from the huge tub to the bed. Soft relaxing music is playing. There's a lot of pain and blood, but it is beautiful. I have never felt as much love in a room. It's the first time in months I'm not thinking about my future or my past. I'm there, present, connected.

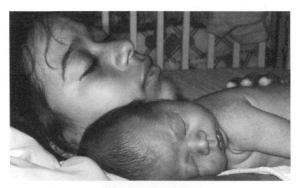

Marina & Kelby.

Kelby is born just before midnight on a Friday night. I spend Saturday with Marina and my new child, but Sunday I'm up in L.A. for the second day of another seminar. Luckily, I have to pay only half-price since I'm there for just one day.

It's a cliché, but I become exactly what my father was to me, exactly what I had promised I'd never be. I'm at the office all of the time. Not only do I have to produce and qualify for my bonus check, but now I have the added pressure of a $2,400-a-month lease.

Rafael and Armando come to help me, and they "buy a desk." To cover the office payments I have to "sell desks" to people who want to have their own key and phone line. I quickly find there are many more expenses in running an office than just the lease payment. Electricity, phone bills, fax machine, cleaning. It all begins to overwhelm me. I work hard rather than smart, putting in continually escalating hours. I've not learned to delegate. Many times I sleep in the office. It saves me the hour-long commute home. If it weren't for Kelby and Marina, I'd probably just live in the office.

During my twelfth month in the business, things click. People sign up. Rafael's doing great. Business is booming. I get a check for $10,064, my first check over ten grand. I've done it. As promised, I take my parents out to dinner. We go to the Hungry Hunter for an early bird special, no plate over $8.95.

That Monday there's a conference call with Bill Gouldd. We're all huddled around the speakerphone.

"How's everybody doing?" All we can hear is static as each office around the country screams into their speakerphone.

"Do you want the good news or the bad news?"

"The bad news!" We've been taught always to ask for the bad news first because then we're left the memory of the good news.

"The bad news is summer sucks! In this industry, summer is the worst time of the year. Everybody's on vacation, they're with their kids. There's no focus or drive in summer. They're the lazy months: June, July, August.

Notice, we don't tell you this at the beginning of summer, but now that it's over. Summer sucks.

"The good news is, it's over." Static again as everybody screams. "And some of you didn't accept the summer excuse. Some of you kept on working and had your best month ever. Rob in Chula Vista, are you there?"

"Yes, Mr. Gouldd. I'm here, sir."

"Rob, are you there?"

"Yes, sir, I'm here!"

"Rob? He's probably out selling a filter."

The mute button is on!

"Sir, I . . . I . . . I'm sorry, I . . . I was here, but my mute button was on. S . . . sorry sir."

"Just another example that anybody can be successful in this business," he chuckles. "Rob, I heard you made over ten thousand dollars last month. How does it feel?"

"Oh, it's incredible sir. I keep following your system, and each month gets better and better. The best thing is, sir, my son was just born and because of your system, I know he'll never have to struggle like I did." I finish out of breath.

"That's why I do what I do. I understand you used to work in the Peace Corps. Did they pay you for that?"

"Not like I get paid here, sir. I could never even dream of making ten thousand dollars in a month before I met you."

"Congratulations, Rob. I'm proud of you. You deserve it."

He talked to me. He congratulated me. He's proud of me. I did it. At twenty-six years old, I've gotten a check for over $10,000. I've opened my own office. I'm my own boss. I'm a dad. Life is good.

The next month, my check is $1,752. Three people have given up their desks, so I'm $1,500 short to cover the rent for the office. I owe the final balloon payment of $3,000 for Kelby's birth. With all my debts and all of the bills I have put off, the $10,000 check is like throwing an Oreo to a T-Rex.

Plus, I need a new car. A top executive like me cannot be seen driving Pegasus. I have to have the right image: a brand-new Honda CRX. I figure I'll be doing a lot of driving, so I get the high-efficiency model, fifty miles to the gallon on the freeway. Friends tell me it has no power. They've never driven Pegasus.

Buying my first new car is an adventure. I walk in with a copy of my $10,000 check, $2,000 cash, and a plan. I'm dressed sharp, and I'm in a hurry. I know if they check my credit, I'll never get the car. So I don't give them time.

"I want to buy the white Honda CRX right there, and I have to leave to catch a plane in thirty minutes. Here's proof of income. I have two thousand dollars cash." I flash the money. "I want to trade in that old car. I'll pay eight thousand dollars out the door. I only have thirty minutes. Can you make it happen?" They're so busy doing the paperwork, they have no time to check my credit report. I drive out thirty minutes later in my first new car.

The next day I start getting messages on my home machine. I hadn't given them a work number. "Mr. Styler, it is extremely important that you return this call." This goes on for about nine days. Finally, we speak on the phone. "Mr. Styler, this is Pacific Honda. The credit department could not approve your loan. We have left you repeated messages over the past week. It seems you've had some credit problems in the past. We need you to return the car immediately."

Living in Guatemala, you can drive from lush, tropical, high-mountain cloud forest to scorching dry desert in one hour. With "the system," you can go from top of the world, financially invincible, to hiding from the repo man in one week.

"I have had some problems," I respond, "and you have a choice. You can see by my report that, at this point, I'm not extremely worried about one more negative mark on my credit. I have the car; you have two thousand dollars and my trade-in. I have already put over a thousand miles on the vehicle. If I bring it back, its value has substantially depreciated. You will have to give me back my two thousand dollars and my trade-in. Your dealership will lose a significant amount of money. Or I can keep the car, make the payments, and you will profit. Worst-case scenario: let's say I don't make the payments. You can repossess the car, you will get to keep the money and my trade-in, and you will still make out better than if I return the car today." They agree with my reasoning.

This is the first of many times when I learn to take control of a situation that before would have left me powerless. The ones I enjoy most are with the bill collectors. I used to feel worthless when I hung up the phone with them. Now it is fun. "Sir, you can see from my credit report that you're not the only person to whom I owe money. I will pay you back. But your threatening, intimidating messages are severely affecting my ability to produce the type of income that will allow me to do that. I've set up a system whereby I'm going to pay back all of my creditors. Would you like to be included in that system?"

"Yes, we would like to be paid the money you rightfully owe us."

"And I want to pay you. Believe me I do. I'm going to pay everybody back, but I'm going to pay the nicest, most respectful people first. No offense personally, but right now you're at the bottom of the list. Either way, you'll get your money. But if you improve your attitude, you will get it much sooner." It works. I begin to learn I'm only powerless when I give away my power.

Since the conference call, I'm considered an expert, a "top producer." People come to me for advice. They want to know how to make the big bucks that I'm making. Whenever associates have me talk to their "new people," I'm introduced as making $10,000 a month. I made $10,000 once. But as with my unprofitable retailing adventures, I say nothing. It feels good to be considered an expert, a top producer. Plus, I don't want to mess up the edification game.

Mr. Gouldd, as always, explains the game well. "How many of you like it when someone talks good about you?" We all yell and whistle. "How many of you like someone who talks good about themselves? Exactly. We all like to be complimented, but if we compliment ourselves, everybody thinks we are egotistical jerks. So here we play the edification game. Edification, for you uneducated folks, is talking good about someone. If I edify you and you edify me, we both get what we want and nobody thinks we're egotistical jerks." More cheering. "At work, what do most people do around the coffee machine? That's right, they talk about whoever is not there. Do they compliment their co-workers and extol their virtues? No, they gossip. 'Did you see what she's wearing? With her legs, I wouldn't have the nerve,' " he says in a mock-female voice. "They tear each other down so they can feel bigger. Here we do the opposite. We build people up. We focus on strengths rather than weaknesses. We edify. Where would you rather spend your time: in a negative, back-stabbing environment, or a positive, motivating environment? Exactly. And that's why we're going to be the fastest growing company in America." Cheers and whistles.

"Also, when you guys work in the office every day, your people know you're not perfect. They know you have bad moods. They know you come late sometimes. They know you're not invincible. But, because they are painfully aware of their own shortcomings, they need someone invincible to believe in, someone they can bet their future on. So we play the edification game.

"You edify them to build their self-confidence, and when somebody edifies you, don't believe it. Don't get all puffed up with yourself. You're still the same scared, insecure person you were when you started. It's like I always say: 'As soon as you forget where you came from, you're on your way back.' The trick to the edification game is to not let your ego get out of whack. When they come to you with stars in their eyes saying how great you are, you then edify your upline, or Sheri Sharman, or Rich Von, or Lori Rubidge, or Marc Accetta.

"These are people who probably aren't in your office every day. Your people don't know their imperfections. I do. They have lots of flaws. But your people will probably never get to know them well enough to find out. When you edify them, they will edify me. Do you understand the game?

There is always somebody bigger and more untouchable for them to believe in. Now, I have imperfections, but I guarantee you they will never know me well enough to find out."

The edification game starts to bother me. I talk to Sheri.

"Everybody keeps edifying me like I'm wealthy, but I'm broke. I'm behind on every bill. I'm behind on the office rent. They might take back the car I just bought. I have to scramble just for gas money, and people are looking at me like I'm a leader. I'm worried I might be leading them to the poorhouse."

"You know what you need to do?" Sheri says.

"What?"

"Buy a Rolex."

"Sheri, I'm not sure if you understood me. I'm broke. I have no money. And you're telling me to buy a ridiculously expensive watch I don't need."

"Exactly."

"Why am I confused here?"

"Rob, you're so focused on where you are, your mind has no blueprint for where you want to go. You need to do something so out of character that your brain gets a wake-up call. If, whenever you look at the time, your brain sees a Rolex, what will that be conveying to your subconscious?"

"Wealth."

"Exactly. Now isn't that what you want to be, wealthy?

Suddenly it all makes sense. I'm broke, so I should buy a Rolex.

My step-dad, Doug, has a harder time following the reasoning. He doesn't think the watch is important, but he knows it is important to me. He says, "I believe in the right of free agency, including making mistakes." He signs the credit application at Bailey, Banks, and Biddle. I now have a two-tone Rolex and a payment of $700 for ten months. I take it one step further and buy a new pair of shoes down in Mexico. I figure I'm broke, but my wrist and my feet don't need to know about it.

It makes a difference. When I strap on my Rolex, slip into my new shoes, put on my double-breasted suit, adjust my silk tie, and hop in my new car, I feel good. I'm reminded of the words of Deepak Chopra:

"Wealth consciousness implies absence of money worries. Go first class all the way and the universe will respond by giving you abundance. Truly wealthy people never worry about losing their money because they know that wherever money comes from there is an inexhaustible supply of it."

At the moment I have no money, but I'm doing my best not to let my subconscious mind know it. The universe must be busy. I'm leaving frantic messages for financial abundance and I only receive more debt.

As my financial situation becomes more desperate, my reputation as a "top producer" and leader continues to grow. This weekend there is another "Millionaire Workshop" seminar. As usual, I'm at the hotel a day early to help set up. I'm now on "full-time staff." I still have to pay for the seminar, but I'm included in special meetings.

Matt Hamilton and I are setting up alone on a Thursday. Matt's a technical wizard who toured with Up With People. Before that he traveled around the Himalayas looking for enlightenment and adventure. Now he's in charge of special effects and sound for Advanced Marketing Seminars. He's creative, funny, and good to work with. I'm technically challenged. He tries to laugh with me rather than at me.

For the big seminars, it takes half of Thursday and then all day Friday to make everything perfect, and Mr. Gouldd demands perfection. With Rafael, the Spanish market has grown considerably, so we now have headsets for simultaneous translation. I'm the translator. My Spanish is good, but it's not perfect. I've never studied it. I learned it in the streets of Guatemala. I can communicate well, but my vocabulary is limited, and my grammar is imperfect. Bill Gouldd speaks quickly, and when he uses a word I can't translate I have to talk around it, which puts me even further behind. Sometimes he'll make a joke, and the Spanish speakers will laugh ten seconds late.

At the big seminars I work a day and a half for free, and then I do the translation Friday night and all day Saturday and Sunday. I pay $495 for this privilege. It doesn't bother me, though. There's an incredible feeling of being involved, connected, important. I'm part of the inner circle.

Bill Gouldd's on a roll: "You guys all want to suck off my energy, off my confidence, off my drive. Success does not come from sucking off my energy, it comes from creating your own. Create your own drive. Create your own confidence." I'm translating all this into Spanish as fast as I can. "Never look beyond yourself for the answer," he continues. "I remember back when I was living in Austin. I had some questions. I knew if I had these questions answered, my business would take off. I called my sponsor and he said if I drove to Houston, he would share some time with me. I drove the two hours to Houston. We sat in a little restaurant, and I asked him my first question. He said, 'What do you think you should do?'

"I looked at him, confused. 'I don't know what to do. That's why I drove two hours out here.'

" 'I can appreciate that, but if you had to come up with an answer, what do you think would be the best solution?'

"We went through twenty questions, and it wasn't until I was cresting the hill going back into Austin that I realized he didn't tell me one thing. I answered all the questions myself. I just did not have the self-confidence to trust myself. I needed someone else to believe in me first. As long as you continue to look outside of yourself for the answers, you'll never be a leader.

"And I'm looking for leaders for my company. I'll tell you one person that has quietly gotten the job done. He's gone out on his own and opened up a new market for the company. He's gone out on his own and opened up a new office. He's the definition of low maintenance. Help me welcome our newest Round Table member, Rob Styler."

I translate, "Roberto Styler." I'm standing with the translation headset on, clapping. Matt pulls my headset off and starts pushing me toward the stage. It's me. I'm a Round Table member. *I am a member of the Round Table.*

More than a thousand people are cheering for me. All I can see are hands and smiles as I run up the aisle. I get to the stage out of breath. Bill Gouldd hands me a microphone, smiles, and walks off stage. People are standing and cheering. I smile broadly with tears in my eyes.

I'm light-headed and still out of breath. I start talking and the crowd quiets.

"At the first 'Basics' I ever went to—it was in Salt Lake City—Bill Gouldd formed the original Round Table. I vowed with everybody else that I would be on it. I didn't really believe I would be, but it was easier to go with the crowd and commit than it was to say I was scared, to say I wasn't sure if I could make it. I'm no longer afraid to admit when I'm afraid. I'll tell you flat out, right now, I'm scared."

The crowd laughs. Feeling them respond is a burst of energy. I give a nervous laugh which sounds like a snort through the speakers.

"If there's one thing I've learned in this business, it's most people live in fear. They're even scared to admit they're scared. What Bill Gouldd has created is a place where we can feel safe to grow beyond our fears, to do what we have always hoped for but never believed possible. At my first "Journey," I wrote my goal to be one of the first twenty people on the Round Table. I am number twenty."

The crowd responds with cheers.

"Each of you deserves to feel what I'm feeling right now. There is such an incredible energy up here with all of you. Thank you for sharing in what, for me, is a dream come true."

People are hugging me, high-fiving, slapping me on the back. My cheeks hurt from smiling so much. I've done it. I'm a Round Table member. I've spoken on stage in front of one thousand people. Bill Gouldd has noticed me.

Becoming a member of the Round Table.

Be humble for you are made of earth. Be noble for you are made of stars.
Serbian Proverb

Chapter 11

You can't escape the responsibility of tomorrow by evading it today.
Abraham Lincoln

I have a special Round Table member pin now. People treat me differently. They seem to look at me like I look at Lori Rubidge or Marc Accetta. It's weird. I'm not saying I don't like it; it's just weird. I feel like Milli Vanilli at the Grammy's before they got caught for lip synching. I have the fame, but I know I don't have the talent.

We're behind on the rent for the office in Chula Vista. Rafael and Armando have gone to Dallas to build the business. Bills are mounting, my bonus checks are small, and I have to uphold the image of a Round Table member.

Bill Gouldd wants to design a satellite system to communicate directly with the offices, but the management for the office complex in Chula Vista won't allow a satellite on the roof. It's a good excuse to leave with dignity. I pay the lease until the day we move out. The office management says I owe them for six more months. They're going to sue me. I tell them to look at my credit and then decide if they want to waste their money in court. Being broke can have its advantages. My first office closes.

I don't want to go back to the same office I started in, but I have to stay in San Diego because I'm still living with my parents. Sheri suggests we need an office in East County. This could work well, because my parents live in East County. No more hour commute. The only problems are that I have no money and I have a broken lease on my already infamous credit report.

The money problem is solved by fate. My parents are in New Zealand for two months on vacation. I'm opening their mail and paying their bills with a little money they left to cover these expenses. I long ago learned to sign my mom's signature.

I open a letter that looks official. It's a check addressed to my mom for $4,800. She didn't tell me about expecting a check, but my grandmother died a few months earlier and it's an inheritance. I figure since my mom didn't mention the check, she wasn't expecting it. They're in New Zealand. They can't use the money. I need the money now. Grandma would want me to have it. Heck, I have seven weeks to earn the money back. I take two deep breaths and sign the check over to myself.

Two days later, I'm in a new office. They check my credit but the broken lease hasn't been reported yet. They also have a lot of suites open. It's the biggest building I've ever seen in East County. It was called the AIDS Building, but they've changed the name for obvious reasons. Now it just has a big 7777 across the top. It's all glass. I get a corner suite on the seventh floor, plush carpet, windows all the way around. I can see the whole city. This is an office.

On pure faith, I sign a three-year lease and give them a $7,500 down payment. I calculate that during the three years, the associates and I will pay over $100,000 for this office. If the level of my success is determined by the level of my commitment, I'm going to be rich.

Lori Rubidge, original Round Table member and top producer, decides to get a desk in my office. This is amazing. I've always dreamed of working with Lori. She's been my patron saint, the one who kept me going, the one who started as slowly as I did. She doesn't get one desk. She buys six. She hands me $3,000 and says, "I'm going to need a place for my new people to work." What a concept. She's so confident, she buys the desks and puts in phone lines before she finds the people. I think of the movie *Field of Dreams*. "Build it, and they will come."

We start building. I'm doing the briefings, and she's closing volume. We make a great team. I watch in awe, trying not to be too obvious. She fills all six desks in the first week.

I've never seen anything like it. There are people everywhere. The briefings are packed. This is the way the business is supposed to work. Lori has a great month. She pulls me aside.

"Rob, I did more personal volume this month than I have in any other month in the company!"

"That's incredible, Lori."

"No, you're incredible. You do the best, most concise, entertaining, informative briefings. All I had to do is get up there and smile. You're amazing. I love working with you. I'm going to tell Mr. Gouldd about this. When he hears how talented you are, you're done. Set for life."

I'm so excited I skip back to my desk. She is the queen of edification. I've never met anyone who can make people feel as wonderful about themselves. I wish I could tape Lori and play it over and over.

Marina and I finally move out of my parents' place. It's hard on them and us. They have bonded with Kelby. They don't kick us out, but they haven't been happy about the check I signed over. Mom makes me reread *The Winter of Our Discontent*. Highlighted and underlined is, "I had thought I could put a process in motion and control it at every turn—even stop it when I wanted. And now the frightening conviction grew in me that such a process may become a thing in itself. . . . What I had done and planned to do was undertaken with full knowledge that it was foreign to me, but necessary as a stirrup is to mount a tall horse." That is all Mom has underlined, yet the next line explains my perspective: "But once I mounted, the stirrup would not be needed."

We move into a one-bedroom apartment within walking distance of the office. Kelby's mobile now and we're on the second floor, so we have to baby-proof everything. I spend little time at home.

We are bringing in so many people to the briefings that our neighbors on the seventh floor have become annoyed. They snidely refer to us as "the water filter people." They are lawyers and accountants, and the fact that we're bursting at the seams, while they have little to no daily business, irritates them.

The elevator's packed, and I'm toward the back. A cute, twentyish woman asks if anybody knows where The Environmental Group is located. I'm about to speak when the lawyer who works next to us says, "Oh, they're on the seventh floor, but you don't want to go there. It's a scam. It's one of those pyramid deals. Don't waste your time."

I decide not to make a scene on the elevator. When the lawyer sees me she becomes visibly nervous. I follow her into her office and say in a stern voice, "That was slander. You know it and I witnessed it. Don't ever slander my business again. I'm going to report this to the building management and may seek legal council." She doesn't say a word. I walk out feeling vindicated and self-important.

The next day I get a letter from the building management.

"We understand you verbally and physically threatened one of our oldest tenants. She is so concerned by your actions that she is afraid to come to work today. This kind of behavior is not acceptable. Because of the large volume of people in and out of your office and your current behavior, your lease is being reviewed by our legal department."

I count to ten and take deep breaths. It's not worth the fight. I decide to let it go. The next week I get another letter from the building management that "several" tenants have complained that we've been using drugs in the office. I tell everybody to go easy on the sage burning.

The volume is way down for the office. Four people have gone off desk. I figure it must be all of the negative energy from the other tenants. I'm alone in the office. It's about midnight and I decide to sage. I mean really sage. I use about four times the normal amount. Smoke is billowing out of the abalone shell. I'm saying the white light prayer and making sure the smoke gets in every corner and crevice of the office. It still doesn't seem like enough so instead of dowsing the sage, I leave it smoking. I set it up so there is no way the smoldering sage could start a fire and I figure, if it smokes all night, any lingering negative energy will be zapped.

The next day I get to the office about 8 A.M. The fire department has been there for an hour. The sage I left smoldering created more smoke than

I could have imagined. There must have been a lot of negative energy in that building. That afternoon we're told we have to leave. My second office closes.

I open up my third office in Santa Ana, more out of habit than excitement. I'm getting better at negotiating and only have to put $2,000 down. It seems all I do is briefings: Spanish, English; English, Spanish. Sometimes I even mix up the two languages. Each day I drag myself to the office. I'm burnt out.

My monthly checks are around $7,000, but my monthly expenses are more. My income is almost entirely because of Rafael's group. I ask Mr. Gouldd what I should do to help Rafael and he says, "Just stay out of his way." That's what Sheri had said.

I'm beginning to hate the business. My attitude becomes cynical. In the office, I'm still jovial and positive, but I don't feel good about what I'm doing. When I first started, it was exciting, a noble quest, helping people and the environment. But too many good people sign up, buy product, go to a few seminars, and then quit three months later. They don't qualify for their check. Sometimes they'll get one good check and then never qualify again; there's no incremental growth. They'll talk about that one good check for six months. They leave broke and embarrassed.

There is a common saying in the business: "Fake it till you make it." I begin to wonder when it ends. I'm a success story, paraded across the stage as an example of what hard work and dedication to this company can bring. But I don't have any money in the bank. I'm still living month to month. Am I leading people down a false path?

When I'm unhappy, I withdraw. I withdraw from Marina. I withdraw from Kelby. I withdraw from the system.

Rafael continues to prosper. It's amazing to witness his growth. He's in his element, in control. My weakest part of the business is closing, or GTC ("get the cash"). Rafael is a master. At the beginning of each month he makes a bunch of fake orders and staples cash to them. When a prospect comes in, he flashes the money and the orders and says, "Look at these orders. They paid cash. They weren't afraid. If you want to be like them, step up, I'll work with you personally. If not, you can work with someone down in my group. I don't have time for people who can't make up their minds." It's effective. He staples about $3,000 in twenty-dollar bills to the orders. It's quite a sight. He works exclusively with the Spanish market, and the flash of the money hypnotizes them to take action and commit.

His most successful student is José Lopez. José is an ex~gang member who now worships Bill Gouldd. Mr. Gouldd did a talk on image. The next day José had the tattoos burned off his hands. Every seminar, José is in the second row, end seat, closest to the middle. A prime chair. I don't know how, but he always gets that seat. His eyes never leave Mr. Gouldd.

I wish I still had his passion. I decide I need a new car. That will motivate me. I page Mr. Gouldd for advice.

"Sir, this is Rob Styler. I want to get a new car and I'm thinking of the Lexus coupe, but I just want to make sure with you that it is a good enough image for the company."

He pages me back, "Lexus coupe is a nice car. Mercedes has a better image. If I were you, I'd get a Mercedes. You do what you want."

All I heard was "Lexus is a nice car. . . . You do what you want." I buy the Lexus. He'd obviously suggested the Mercedes. I use the same trick for the purchase. I'm in a hurry, show copies of my best checks, give them $7,000 cash and drive off. They don't have time to check my credit.

At the next seminar I cringe, knowing he's talking about me.

He begins, "What really pisses me off is when some of you top producers call me for advice, I give it to you, and then you do exactly what you wanted to do in the first place. How do you think that makes me feel?"

I'm not sure how he feels, but I know the Lexus doesn't seem like such a great car anymore.

The office has become my prison instead of my cocoon. I escape any chance I can. My lunches become longer and I eat alone. I sneak off to matinees. Anything to be out of the office.

On one of my escapes, I spend two days with my parents. They've moved. Eight years ago they bought a piece of land in Ramona, and now they've built their dream home. Talking with my parents always grounds me. They provide perspective.

"Rob, if it feels like the right thing to be doing, keep doing it. But if you're just doing it for the money, it's time to leave," my mom shares.

I'm driving home down Wildcat Canyon, thinking. I'm driving fast, but not recklessly. Last night was the first rain of the season, so the road is slick. I come around one of my favorite corners, and I see a squirrel in the middle of the road. I react, slamming on the brakes. The car goes into a spin, hits the curb, and flies off a thirty-foot cliff. I'm calm as I spin around, first on the pavement and then in the air. The car lands on all four wheels at the bottom of the cliff. I look at my body—everything is there, no blood.

The air bags didn't inflate. The tape deck is still playing. It's Mr. Gouldd's voice, a tape from a "Journey" seminar: "It doesn't matter how many times you get knocked down in life. It's how many times you get up that matters." The man has timing even on tape. I start laughing. A woman whose house I almost landed on looks at me like I'm drunk or on drugs.

"Are you okay?"

"Yeah, I'm fine."

"What happened?"

"Squirrel."

It becomes infamous in the company as "the squirrel story." Mr. Gouldd says, "Rob's the only top producer in the company who would destroy a $40,000 automobile rather than kill a squirrel."

There's over $20,000 in damage and both of the axles are broken in the crash, but my Lexus is "repaired." It doesn't ride the same. I complain to the insurance company and get nowhere. Each month I reluctantly send in my $700 lease payment.

Marina, Kelby, and I are now living with Marina's brother and his family on the lake where Rafael slept before his first seminar. We live in a little room with aluminum walls that bakes in the summer and freezes in the winter. But they're friendly, we have a view of the lake, and it's rent-free.

It's ironic: my shiny new Lexus parked in front of our trailer home. People don't see where I live, but they see what I drive. Image.

> *None are more hopelessly enslaved than those*
> *who falsely believe they are free.*
>
> Goethe

Chapter 12

If one is out of touch with oneself, then one cannot touch others.
Anne Morrow Lindbergh

I continue my downward cycle. I'm excited and motivated during the briefings and trainings, but away from "the system," I'm isolated and alone. My marriage deteriorates. Marina has been a trooper. She married a Peace Corps volunteer who wanted to live on a farm in Guatemala. Now she's living with a manic-depressive capitalist who's surviving through denial.

Because I'm unavailable, Marina, in the Latin way, surrounds herself with family. Now when I'm home, when I need solitude, it's loud and crowded.

I escape for three days to Doug's family cabin near Lake Tahoe to think and spend time in nature. Instead I get sick, really sick. Fortunately, my brother Rick is a chiropractor and holistic healer.

"Bro, fix me," I say weakly.

"You look like shit."

"Thanks for the bedside manner." It hurts to smile.

"Let me test you." Rick runs through a series of neuro-emotional techniques. These tests determine the emotional, physical, and chemical strengths of each organ and function in my body. He's spending a lot of time and is becoming obviously concerned.

"Bro, I can't believe how toxic you are. Every organ and function I've tested is shot. You're killing yourself. I know the way you are. You're mono-focused. This is the first time in two years you've given your body the permission and time it needs to heal. It's taking this window of opportunity and cleaning house. You're going through a major spontaneous detox. Your body's screaming what you haven't wanted to see. You need to make some serious lifestyle choices."

Rick's right. I'm not happy. I do none of the things that used to bring me joy. I've stopped jogging. I don't read like I used to. I haven't been backpacking in two years. I can't remember the last time I watched a sunset. This is the first vacation I've had since I answered the ad. By working desperately for financial freedom, I've created a lifestyle with no finances and no freedom.

That weekend I decide to get a divorce. I think Marina is relieved in a way. I haven't been a husband or a father for two years. This makes it official.

Kelby is two years old. He pushes both of us inside the bathroom and closes the door. We don't resist. We can hear him lean against the door, crying. Marina and I make a commitment. Though our marriage will end, Kelby is the priority.

As my marriage is ending with Marina, another divorce is happening. Bill Gouldd is leaving NSA and taking us with him. He always made sure our loyalty was to him and Advanced Marketing Seminars: "Manufacturers are easy to find. What we have is a distribution system. Products come and go. Marketing is eternal. How many of you think if you go into a supermarket in ten years they'll have all the same products on the shelves? Of course not. Products change. But the supermarket will still be there. We're the supermarket. We can market any product."

In October 1991 Bill Gouldd leaks the news to a small group of us. "We've been making NSA millions of dollars and they've treated us like shit. I'm sick of it. This water filter sucks!" He holds up a cross-section of the filter, showing the inner structure. "It's a piece of PVC pipe filled with carbon and then capped and held together with carcinogenic glue. It probably costs them less than five dollars to produce this piece of shit. I'm embarrassed we've been selling this crap. In January we're starting our own company. We're going to do it right. It's going to be called Consumer Direct International."

We're all in shock but for different reasons. I can't believe I've been selling a "piece of shit" for two years. My friends and family have this piece of shit on their sinks. I've told them it would protect their health, that it was the best water filter on the planet. They believed me. I believed me. I've been unknowingly lying to people for two years.

We're going to announce the switch in Denver in January 1992. Word leaks to the field and people are excited: our own company, our own deal. Bill Gouldd is going to do it right.

Before the big rally, we have a small meeting of the "top people." Everybody's excited. I'm nauseous. I haven't sold one filter or signed up one person for two months. Our job was to keep the momentum going before the switch. I've let him down. Mr. Gouldd starts the meeting angry.

"Some of you guys have done a tremendous job these last two months. Some of you assholes took a shit in my living room. What the fuck happened to you, Rob? I ask you to produce—two months was all I asked. And you fucking crawl into your shell. You haven't done shit in two months." He pauses. "Well, talk."

"I . . . I just can't sell something I don't believe in."

"You've believed in and sold the same filter for two years."

"That's before I knew it was a piece of shit."

"Who the fuck told you it was a piece of shit?"

"You did, sir."

Everybody waits to see his reaction. He hates when anybody uses his own words against him.

He laughs, "That's right, I did." Everybody laughs nervously. "Okay, Rob, you're excused. I forgot how fucking socially conscious you are." People chuckle at this. I'm known as the squirrel-saving, vegetarian, ex~Peace Corps volunteer. "But the rest of you fuckers have no excuse. You're just waiting. I ask you to cover my back and you're only concerned about your future. If you take care of my future, your future will be handled. All I ask is five years. If you will dedicate the next five years of your lives to building this company, I will reward you beyond your wildest imaginations. You will experience wealth unimaginable. We will create a worldwide marketing force more powerful than any system in history. We will impact and improve more people's lives than any system in history.

"Each of you in this room has a chance to go down in history as being one of the original people, one of the pioneers of change. It's going to be hard the first twelve months. Some of you aren't going to make it. We're making this switch four months premature. We're giving birth to a preemie. We're not ready. We don't have product yet. I need to know if I can count on each of you to keep the dream alive, keep the troops on fire. No questions. No doubt. Five years. You commit five years to me. That's all I ask, five years for wealth and world impact. Can you do it?"

"Yes!" We're excited, delirious. Five years to wealth and worldwide impact.

About four thousand people come to the rally in Denver. Most are excited. Some are in shock. They just bought $5,000 worth of NSA water filters. We're thankful the new name isn't Consumer Direct. (None of us liked that name, but we were too scared to tell the Big Guy.) We're now Equinox International.

For the first three months, we have no product. But we're selling; we're selling the dream. I'm doing briefings, drawing on the whiteboard what the filter is going to look like, and people are giving me money so they will be the first ones to receive product once we have it. I'm enthusiastic. I believe. People want to be a part of it.

It's taking longer than planned to develop the real water filter we're going to market. We need something. We place a private label on another manufacturer's filter. We're selling it for $200. Price Club has the exact same filter for $89. People are starting to quit. It's a hard year. My third office closes. I have no money and have to pawn my Rolex to pay child support.

I'm at another "Perpetual Money Machine" seminar. It's amazing how it has grown. At the first one I went to in 1990, Evonne Hoffler sewed Bill Gouldd's costumes, and he went behind a cheap curtain to change. Now millions of dollars are spent on the sets and costumes, sixty people work backstage, and it puts most Hollywood productions to shame.

The concept is that we learn best from stories and entertainment, not facts and lectures. When prompted, we can all remember a song or catchy ad phrase we haven't heard since high school. Bill Gouldd got the idea from the movie *Fletch Lives*. He dresses up in different costumes with different backdrops to teach success concepts in an entertaining story format. It works. Whenever I'm in a difficult situation and I need perspective, I think of the Golfer, or the Fisherman, or the Construction Worker, or the Doctor, or my favorite, the Farmer.

During one of the breaks, a beautiful, dark-skinned woman walks up to me. "Hi, I'm Seana. I understand you have a video of Spanish testimonials. I could really use a copy in Santa Barbara. Do you know how I can get one?"

"You live up in Santa Barbara?" I ask, trying not to sound excited.

"Yep, lived there my whole life."

"I grew up in Santa Barbara. I'm going there next weekend for my ten-year high school reunion."

"No way." She looks at me in disbelief. "My high school reunion is next week. What high school did you go to?"

"Santa Barbara High." We laugh. We went to the same high school, graduated the same year, and never knew each other. We've met ten years later. I think it is fate.

I get to Santa Barbara a day early to do a briefing and to see Seana. I walk in the office and there she is, sitting behind the front desk. At least I think it's her. Wow, she looks way older. It must have been dark at the seminar. Nice looking lady, but she looks middle-aged. How could I have graduated from high school with her?

Confused, I say, "Hey, good to see you."

"I've heard a lot about you," she says. Now I'm more confused.

I'm about to ask for an explanation when Seana walks in from the side door and introduces me to her mom, Juanita. I exhale. Seana is just as beautiful and young as I remember.

Our high school reunion is an ego boost. I was skinnier, stuttered more, and had acne in high school. I was self-conscious and desperately wanted to belong. I had a great group of friends, but not high self-esteem. At the reunion, I discover most of the people who intimidated me in high school have not evolved. They still "party" and get drunk. I see worn, tired souls. I know I'm depressed, but some of these people look desperate. By comparison, I feel better.

Seana and I begin a relationship, and I decide to move to Santa Barbara to work my "warm market." I move in with Seana and her mom. We're working hard at the office, but I'm just going through the motions. It's difficult to be the "expert" when I've no passion for what I'm doing.

My results reflect my passion. I struggle and again escape in illness. I cannot even get out of bed for two weeks. Seana takes care of me. I need to be taken care of.

We decide to get our own apartment in Orange County. It's a rocky relationship. We have different values, and both of us are stressed. Seana had been successful in fashion retail and is now broke and struggling with Equinox. She gets a part-time job as a waitress at the Cheesecake Factory. We combine our finances.

At the next "Leadership" seminar, Mr. Gouldd is pissed. He's not at all happy with our leadership. Friday night we have a special meeting with all of the Round Table members. The room is tense as we wait for him to come down to dinner. We talk in whispers. He walks in, doesn't say hello to anyone, and walks straight to the microphone.

"All of you fuckers are ruining my company. I put you in leadership positions. I thought you could handle it. You all got so impressed with yourselves that you think you're too good to work, too good to take an ad call, too good to get to the office early. I'm sick of it. You know why we have double-doors on a lot of the briefing rooms? It's so some of you can get your egos through the door." We're all too scared to laugh.

"All of you 'leaders,' you 'top producers,' are taking a shit in the middle of my company. I make you a member of my inner circle, put you on the Round Table. I give you a pin so everybody will look up to you. And what do they see when they look up? Lazy, unproductive, egotistical assholes.

I'm sick of it. Turn in your pins."

A glass bowl is handed around. We each drop our Round Table pin in the bowl as it passes by. He waits. Each one makes a distinctive "chink" as it hits the bowl or the other pins. It reminds me of a Sprint commercial.

"Okay, that done, we need to get this shit working. We need to find some solutions. Give me ideas. What can we do to get production up to where it should be?" We're silent. We're all hoping someone else will talk. He gets more hostile when we don't respond. The hotel staff stops serving the meal and leans against the wall. I imagine them thinking, *I don't get paid much, but I'm glad I'm not them.* The higher I move up in the company, the further I get from HappyLand.

"Now you're not going to talk to me. Did I hurt your feelings? Okay, I still like you." I read once that violently abusive husbands have a pattern of beating their wives and then telling them how much they love them. "If you guys are going to crawl into your shells, I'm going to leave. Somebody better talk to me."

Chris Rowland raises his hand. "Mr. Gouldd, there's a long wait on hold to get through to representative support. Maybe we could have a special phone line for Execs and International Marketing Directors so we could be more productive and not have to spend so much time waiting on the phone." Wrong answer. Chris is sitting about ten feet away. Mr. Gouldd grabs a biscuit and wings it straight at Chris's head. It catches him across the face. Chris holds back tears, more from shock and humiliation than pain.

Mr. Gouldd resumes his tirade. "This is the exact kind of shit I'm talking about. Rather than thinking of the field, you fuckers think of yourselves. Chris, how about we get you your own fucking office with a private secretary who can make your calls for you? That way you won't have to do a fucking thing.

"I know what the problem is: You fuckers want to be like me. Because I don't work in an office, you think you no longer need to. I've got news for you. You aren't me—not even close. You try to buy the same cars I buy. You try to find the same watch I have. Do me a favor. Let me be me, and you be you. At least you're not copying my hairstyle anymore." We laugh nervously. When Mr. Gouldd had a perm, several men got matching perms. It was ridiculous. "If you buy my car, I have to buy a better one. If you buy my watch, I have to buy a better one. You can't afford my watch. Let me be a level above you. I am a level above you."

We all stare at him. He laughs. "I can even throw a biscuit better than you." He whips a biscuit across the room. "Come on, aren't you going to defend yourselves?" Biscuits start flying from everywhere. Our nervous energy is transformed into a food fight.

From then on at our company events, we can always tell the new people, the ones who just got promoted. They eat their rolls. After the "biscuit incident," we save our ammo.

I open my fourth office in Newport Beach with Seana. It's a small office with low rent, but there's a great garden and big trees. It's homey. I like it.

I'm about to start the briefing when a large man in overalls asks to speak with me. The office is packed with people waiting to see the briefing. Kindly, he leads me to a private room.

"I need you to sign this." He hands me a clipboard.

"What am I signing?" I am confused.

"We're taking your car."

"Where? Why?"

"To the repossession lot because you haven't made a payment in three months."

"What if I give you a check right now?" I even have the money in my account.

He laughs. "Sorry, it's passed that stage. You just have to sign."

"Well, can you wait until I finish the briefing? I'm running a business."

"So am I. Sorry."

People can see my car being jacked up and hauled away outside. Some of the associates are concerned. I tell them not to worry. What am I going to say? I have to do the briefing. What would Bill Gouldd do? I know. Find the positive—look at it from a different angle. Don't lie, but selectively tell the truth. I walk to the front of the room.

"You know, I love this business. It used to be that when I had a car problem, I had to waste half the day at the garage reading old magazines. Now they come straight to my office. I'll never have to worry about that car." And I didn't. The only bummer was my special rhino pin is in the glove compartment. I never get it back.

After six months, we finally have the real deal, the best water filter in the world: three stages, four media, and ABS food-grade plastic ultrasonically welded together. The best.

The problem is our manufacturer is in such a hurry to rush the filters out, they aren't properly field-tested. The ultrasonic welds don't hold. It's like Russian roulette: In each order, one filter explodes. They start to slowly leak and then they split open, spewing water and carbon all over the kitchen. The worst are the shower units. The whole faceplate pops off, whacks customers on the head, and dumps carbon all over them.

By the end of the first year, out of the thousand people I brought over from NSA, forty are left. I still have a thousand people in my sales force, but they're all new people. It's a hard year.

The stress is mirrored in my relationship with Seana. I'm not happy. I talk about breaking up. She's extremely upset. I can't handle the stress caused by my proposed breakup, so I propose marriage.

We send $50 to the Universal Life Church so Bill Gouldd can be the minister. Sheri Sharman lets us have the wedding at her house. Imo and Lori Rubidge are there. Mark Soda is taking pictures. It's an Equinox wedding. My parents aren't happy but respect my right of free agency.

Bill Gouldd is late as usual. He is the person who is supposed to marry us, and he gets to Sheri's house fifteen minutes late wearing shorts and a T-shirt. He goes downstairs to change and we wait. After fifteen more minutes, I go down and he is watching football.

"Mr. Gouldd, this is my day, not your day. You can be late to your seminars, but you have no right to make me wait for my wedding." My tone shocks him and me. I look in his eyes and see a scolded little boy. For an instant the shield comes down. But we quickly remember our roles. I am again respectful. He is again arrogant.

"Rob, you can still say no. Just don't do it. Nobody will think any less of you. Marriage sucks—one woman the rest of your life. You know the similarities between a tornado and marriage, don't you?" I try to smile as I shrug my shoulders. "At the beginning there is a whole lot of blowing and sucking, and when it's all over, you lose the house."

I am not in the mood for jokes, but I smile and ask him to please hurry. Walking back upstairs I see his eyes as the scolded child each time I blink. That moment was the first time I ever saw him unguarded, vulnerable.

I am off-balance the rest of the day. Seana and I are not the right match. Everybody sees it. Even I see it, but it seems less stressful to go forward than back.

Seana, Rob, and Lori Rubidge

Six months later we're divorced. Seana has become a co-applicant of my distributorship, so we divide the sales force. She's moved to my front level and four of our Directors move beneath her. My only stipulation is that I keep Rafael. She picks Dr. Cohn, who hasn't done much in the business yet. He's busy running his growing chiropractic office.

I'll never forget when we first met Dr. Cohn. Seana had taken me to his health class.

"Maybe we can recruit the doctor," she said. We got there and he was talking about environmental health. I raised my hand. "Excuse me, but I work with a company called Equinox and we solve many of the problems you're discussing." Dr. Cohn, or Howie as his friends call him, was interested until he found out it's a network marketing company. The red flags went up. I backed off and started concentrating on the free food.

Since then, Howie has become a friend, and his interest in the business has grown. We encourage Meagan, his secretary and girlfriend, to sign up with Equinox. We spend New Year's Eve at Howie's place watching the boat parade in Newport Beach.

As part of Howie's practice, he offers an intense neural-emotional session to work through personal blocks and issues. For $300 I decide to give it a try.

"Rob, you have a block with money. You don't think you deserve to make more than about seventeen thousand a month. You're keeping yourself back." He doesn't know it, but my biggest check so far is $17,400. I'm intrigued.

"Well, get rid of it and earn your three hundred dollars."

He laughs. "See, there's that money issue." He works with me and finds I have a scarcity issue with money. I think if I have more, someone else must have less. I've been subconsciously sabotaging my success. It all seems pretty wild, but the next month I make over $21,000. He becomes my healer and a good friend.

There's a big event for all of the Execs and International Marketing Directors at Mr. Gouldd's Colorado ranch. I get to be in nature, walking under the pines, breathing fresh air.

Seana and I stay close during the divorce and decide to stay together in the cabins. Mr. Gouldd hears about this at dinner and is not happy. Unfortunately, I'm sitting directly across from him. "Rob, what the fuck is your problem? You don't feel like a whole man unless you have a woman holding your dick." I've learned that it's better not to say anything when he's in one of these moods. Dinner doesn't taste good, though.

The ranch is like I've dreamed: panoramic vistas, walking trails, horses, rustic cabins, lakes filled with fish. We actually have a contest to see if anybody can cast all the way out and reel back so fast as not to catch a trout. The day is idyllic. The evening is eye-opening.

We're sitting around the fire and Mr. Gouldd is in one of his moods to reestablish his position as the Alpha dog. None of us question his authority; sometimes he just feels the need.

"I could get any one of you kicked out of the company at any time for any reason." We all stop eating and look at him.

"Rob." *Why me?* "We have to kick somebody out. It's going to be either you or Seth. Who would you prefer?"

"Seth," I answer cautiously.

"Good answer. Now we need some dirt on Seth to get him out. If you can't provide it, we have to kick you out. Your choice."

I'm trying to read if he's joking or not. I'm feeling uncomfortable, so I try to joke. "You know, I've been meaning to call you about Seth. He's been doing some wild stuff and . . . "

"You get my point," Mr. Gouldd interrupts me. "I could get shit on any one of you fuckers at any time. Even if I couldn't get any dirt on you, I could still just kick you out. What could you do, sue me? I would stop your check. You'd have no money coming in. My lawyers would tie you up in court for years. You would not even have money to eat. You could forget about hiring lawyers. You would be broke before you started." He pauses and looks at each of us. "Point being: Don't piss me off."

I look at the dirt. I don't feel whole.

A change came o'er the spirit of my dream.
Lord Byron

Chapter 13

It's only possible to live happily ever after on a moment-to-moment basis.

Margaret Bonnano

I'm divorced—again. I don't have a place to live. Seana gets the car because her dad signed for it. Neither of us has any credit left. I make good money, but I spend it all and more. I get a check for $18,000, and it's gone in three weeks. I don't live extravagantly. But the expenses continue to build: office, ads, phones, travel, product, seminars. The system consumes whatever I produce.

I escape to Atlanta. It's far away, and I have a group working there. I make a little money and buy a new Rolex. I have to keep the image.

I'm flying "home" when I realize I don't have a home or a car. I pay child support to Marina, and I'm still paying alimony to Seana. Marina has remarried and has a new baby, Kevin. Finances are tight, so I figure we should pool our resources.

We all move in together: Marina and her new husband Juan, their son Kevin, Seana and her mom, Kelby, and me.

We get along great, but I feel like I should be on *The Oprah Winfrey Show*: "Husbands Who Live With Both Their Ex-Wives . . . One unique case, Rob Styler, even lives with his first ex-wife's husband, their new child, and the mother-in-law of his second marriage, plus his son and both his ex-wives. You'll get to meet Rob after this commercial break."

I keep my parents entertained with all my adventures. They keep me sane. Doug thinks it's ridiculous but I come up with the down payment and he signs the credit application for my new Jaguar.

I begin to develop more of a relationship with Kelby. He is now four. Kelby receives a lot of love from Marina and my parents, and it's hard for me to believe how accepting and loving he is toward me. Marina is a good mom. Kelby's an incredible child. Through his eyes I begin again to remember the wonder of a creek bed, the fascination of watching tadpoles evolve. I love to make him laugh. He has a wonderful laugh.

After six months of rooming with everybody, I move into my own apartment. Reflecting my mood, I find a ridiculously expensive, one-bedroom apartment in Irvine with gray walls and steel bars everywhere.

My paychecks have gone down, but my expenses are still as high. I'm sleeping on the floor and have no furniture. My fourth office closes. This is the only one of the four in which I actually finish the lease. I even get my deposit back.

In January it's time for Equinox's 1995 kick-off celebration. Awards are given. New products are introduced. We hear wonderful speakers. The seminar ends with an amazing concert by Kenny Loggins. The top fifty people are all up on stage for the grand finale. It's powerful. Looking out from the stage over the crowd of eight thousand people, I'm reminded why we started, what the vision was. Giving people a higher purpose and meaning in their lives. That's what gave me passion. How did that vision become so distant, so clouded?

I'm walking out through the sea of bodies. It's a weird feeling. Whenever I'm at a big seminar, I can hear people whispering as I walk by, "That's Rob Styler. He's an International Marketing Director and trainer." I feel self-conscious and look straight ahead.

A petite, beautiful woman comes up to me. "Hi, my name is Val Michels. I always wanted to meet you. You taught my first 'Basics.' "

"So I was your first," I say jokingly.

"You could say that." She doesn't have the same overly peppy, false enthusiasm of most people in Equinox. She's not "under the ether." I want to keep talking.

We eat dinner before she has to catch a plane back to Seattle. I steal a quick kiss at the airline gate.

That night I leave a message on her machine. I send flowers the next day. I haven't been as excited about a woman, about anything, in years.

I convince her to fly down to go to a four-day spiritual seminar I'm planning to attend next weekend. I'll pay for the seminar if she pays for the flight. I'm up front with her, and I tell her my mom's rule. "As you know, Val, I've been divorced twice, so my mom gave me a guideline. I can sleep with you; I just can't marry you." She laughs and says she wants to meet my mom.

Val flies down to get to know this man she just met who is a "top producer" in the company she recently joined. I'm living in a one-bedroom cell with no furniture, sleeping on the floor. To her credit, she doesn't say anything.

The seminar is wonderful, and so is she. I'm swept off my feet. She's everything I'm looking for in a partner. She has dinner at my parents', the big test. She gets the highest grade: "We'd like to see her a lot more, Rob."

The more excited I get, the more I notice she's not. Over the next four months she begins to pull away. I fly up to Seattle, and at the airport it's obvious something is wrong.

"Rob, I'm just not ready for a big commitment. I've recently ended a four-year relationship. You've been divorced less than a year. I'm looking for relationship-lite. You're a double espresso of commitment." I just look at her. "Plus, I met somebody else."

That night I'm sleeping on the couch. Val doesn't know how thin her walls are because I can hear her quietly flirting with "somebody else" on the phone in the next room. It's a hard week.

Rather than wallow deeper in my depression, I start to work on me. I begin that morning to do the little things that bring me joy. Each morning as I'm running, I see the same three elderly ladies. They've been walking every day together for five years. Each rendezvous we talk a little more. By the end of the week they know the whole story. They each promise I'll meet the right woman at the right time.

I'm reading *Chicken Soup for the Soul* at night before I go to bed. There's a story about celebrating the little things, the special moments, the special people. On my last day I give each of the ladies a bouquet of flowers and say thank you. We're all touched, especially me.

I hate my one-bedroom cell and I miss living with Kelby, so I rent a big five-bedroom house in Irvine. We all move in. This time it's just Marina, Juan, Kevin, Kelby, and me. It works great. I get to see my son every day.

I've been a paid trainer with Advanced Marketing Seminars for two years now. It's what I enjoy most. It's the only part of the business that feels natural and comfortable. It's ironic that what had created panic, because of my stuttering, now feels second nature. Sheri told me, "If you can turn your fear into your career, you've accomplished something profound."

When I teach a "Basics" I feel I accomplish something, like I am able to share words that make a difference. It's not that I teach any great truisms. I'm just honest. I tell people how hard I've struggled, and it makes their struggles more bearable.

There's another big seminar this weekend. At least as a trainer I get to go for free. There's also a level of intrigue this weekend because a young lady I've wanted to know is going to be there.

The seminar is packed as always. I maneuver through the crowd in her direction and position myself directly in her path. Like basketball, the trick is to cut off the passing lanes.

"Mr. Styler, it's great to see you again." Plan A works. She initiates contact.

"What's this Mr. Styler stuff? You make me feel old. Call me Rob."

"It's just out of respect. Isn't this exciting? This weekend's going to be awesome!" *It's looking better all the time.*

"Yeah, isn't this company amazing? I'm just glad to be part of it."

"Me, too," she responds.

"LADIES AND GENTLEMEN, WILL YOU PLEASE TAKE YOUR SEATS. MR. GOULDD IS ABOUT TO BEGIN."

"I'll see you later," I say hopefully.

"That'd be great."

I go to my reserved seat in the front row, and Khristina moves several rows back. There are about three thousand people in the room.

The lights are dimmed slightly to encourage everyone to take a seat. Then it's completely black. A few cheers and whistles scatter through the crowd, new people. A small background light shows an eerie smoke spreading across the stage. The smoke rolls into the first few rows. Several people start coughing from the gas. It smells almost sweet. The music starts and the words and images for the song are displayed on two thirty-foot screens.

The song ends and laser lights from the rear begin to twirl across the stage. The stage is set up like a giant chessboard receding off into infinity, continuing to narrow until it becomes a point on the backdrop. From that exact point, another laser light twirls out into the crowd, creating wild images in the smoke. There are six-foot high pawns, ten-foot bishops, and giant rooks. Suddenly the king begins to rotate and there, sitting inside the king, is Bill Gouldd.

The crowd explodes with cheers and applause. He waits for the crowd to quiet. But they keep screaming. He keeps waiting. They keep screaming. He motions his hand downward and they stop. It reminds me of a scene from *Malcolm X* where he points his finger to the right, the troops march off in formation, and the policeman says, "No one should have that much power."

Bill Gouldd stares across the crowd. "How many of you've been pawns your whole life? Letting somebody else control the game as you go through the motions. All you see is survival because you're used to subsisting on scraps. You cling to security but the more you desire security, the less you have. What's the first thing that comes to your mind when you think *maximum security?* That's right: prison. And that's exactly where most of you have been living your whole life. You're in prison without bars. You work a job you hate but are too scared to leave. Your life is controlled by one thing, *fear.* I'm still mad I didn't think of those 'No Fear' stickers." The crowd laughs. "Our society is consumed by fear. You have two choices:

Live your dreams, or live your fears."

I've heard so many variations on this theme over the years that it doesn't have the same impact. The day continues in the same direction. He's in one of his moods. Angry at the world and in a position to let everyone know about it. We listen, some inspired, others offended, all confronted.

Toward the end of the day, he starts hammering on the leadership. We all sit up straight, extra attentive. Each of us pretends to be wondering whom he could be talking about and scared to death we are next.

"If I hear one more complaint about George pinching some girl's ass, not only am I going to kick you out of the company, George, but I'll file criminal charges. Do you understand me?" The camera zooms in on George's face. I am sitting ten feet from him, but I look up on the thirty-foot screen. There is hate in his eyes as he slowly nods.

Mr. Gouldd breathes out a laugh. "I bet you couldn't squeeze a toothpick up the asshole of one person in the front row right now." We all laugh, nervously.

"If you 'leaders' would just quit chasing away every good-looking woman who comes into this company, we could break more records. You're all focused on volume, and then a hot-looking woman comes into the office, and your blood pressure drops to your waist. Some of you ladies are just as guilty. We call the guys studs, and we call the girls something else."

I'm always amazed at what he will say in front of three thousand people. He continues, "If you guys can just focus on building the business and keep your dicks in your pants for a few years you'll be able to get more than you can even imagine today." He looks across the front row and stops at me. I stop breathing. "Here, Rob, I have something for you, Equinox hand and body lotion." He tosses me a bottle. "I heard you have a problem with this. Whenever you get the urge, just grab this bottle. You know how there are heterosexuals, homosexuals, and bisexuals? I want you to be an autosexual." I just stare at him. "Could somebody in the back make sure corporate sends Rob a case of hand and body lotion? It's on me. In fact, maybe we should just send a case to all the leadership. Volume would probably double."

Why did he pick me? I've slept with one woman in the past year. I have never been a player. The seminar ends to loud music. I'm so embarrassed that I haven't heard the last hour. I get up and leave the bottle of lotion under my seat.

I want to find Khristina but have no idea what to say. We were definitely flirting. Now she probably thinks I'm a playboy.

"So, was I going to be the flavor of the week?" There's my answer.

"No, Khristina. I don't know why he said that. He could have picked anyone. It just happened to be me."

"So you're trying to convince me it was just random. Out of all of the guys in the front row he just happened to pick you. Pure chance."

"I know it looks bad. I don't know what to say. I am attracted to you. I was hoping to get to know you better this weekend. I think you're attracted to me, also. If you want, ask people who know me. I'm not a playboy."

She smiles and tilts her head. "Okay, I would like to get to know you, too."

We set a date for that Wednesday night. We plan to meet at a restaurant on the beach halfway between Orange County, where I live, and San Diego, where she lives.

I get there a half-hour early. I'm always early. I figure it's better that I wait than somebody else. Khristina is late.

She's wearing a short black skirt and a silk blouse. She looks good. I'm reminded of what Mr. Gouldd said about blood pressure dropping to my waist.

Dinner's great. We have a quiet corner table overlooking the water and sunset. She's visibly nervous. I continually compliment her, and she begins to relax.

We walk out on the pier arm in arm. I look down and can see the curve of her breast beneath the silk. We lean against the railing and look down on the water. I kiss her and she responds. Wow, does she respond. No nervousness here. *Intense* is more the word. We kiss hard for about five minutes, and then she pulls away.

"What's wrong?"

"I'm dizzy." She smiles, looking down at the ground. "I've been dating the same man for four years. I haven't kissed anybody but him since I was nineteen. This is just so much."

"Yeah, that was pretty intense."

"Don't get me wrong; it felt great. I'm just confused."

"About what?"

"I just don't think I'm ready."

This would have stopped me cold in high school or college, but now Bill Gouldd has trained me. If someone says no and you try convincing her, she naturally resists, the wall gets thicker, and she thinks you're pushy. So you have to take a different angle. Never try to beat down the wall of resistance when you can simply walk around it.

"What's your favorite ice cream?"

"What?"

"Your favorite ice cream, what flavor is it?"

"Chocolate." She smiles. Everybody loves ice cream. Nobody likes pressure.

"Chocolate is great, isn't it? You've probably eaten a lot of chocolate ice cream during your life haven't you?"

"Yeah."

"If you ate way too much chocolate ice cream all the time, it might get boring. You might not even want to eat any more ice cream, right?"

"Yeah, I think I know what you're talking about."

"Have you ever been to Italy?"

"No." She's completely confused now.

"There is a little gelato shop in Florence, close to the statue of David. It has been there for fifty years, a small, family-run place. They make a raspberry gelato that's amazing. One of the brothers has a farm high in the Alps where the raspberries grow sweet in the mountain sun. They make the gelato by hand with a recipe that has been handed down generation to generation. The first time I tasted it, I couldn't believe the flavor. It was incredible; completely different than anything I'd tasted before. I went back nine times for more during the two days I spent in Florence."

I've connected ice cream, foreign travel, and frequent sex in one appealing package. "Now, you've been eating chocolate ice cream for the last four years. You're saying you're not sure if you're ready to eat any more ice cream, but the only flavor you've known is chocolate."

"So what are you saying?"

"Try the gelato."

She smiles.

> *But what a woman says to her lusting lover it is best to*
> *Write in wind and swift-flowing water.*
> Catullus

Chapter 14

A State which dwarfs its men, in order that they may be more docile instruments in its hands even for beneficial purposes, will find that with small men no great things can really be accomplished.
John Stuart Mill

Two weeks later, Khristina moves in with "the family." Oprah could do a sequel. Khristina has no money, so I hire her as my personal assistant. We start building the business.

Something is missing. I'm working too hard for the limited results I'm receiving. The majority of my check is still because of Rafael's group. People sign up, get excited, and then quit. I've been doing this for more than four years—when will it end? When does the steady residual income start?

I still have to struggle to qualify for all my bonuses. Each month I have to sell $5,000 worth of wholesale inventory. We have one of the hardest qualifications for monthly bonuses in the industry. I bring this up to Mr. Gouldd on an Executive conference call and he says, "If the qualifications are any easier, people will just work less, you spineless wimp." I can see his point, but when the qualifications are too hard, people just quit.

I wonder if it's only in my group. Maybe I'm doing something, or not doing something, that's creating my perpetual exodus. Explaining my situation, I ask other top people for advice. They have the same situation, the same problem.

My doubts about "the system" begin to grow. Mr. Gouldd is the most talented person I've ever met in this industry. I think it's hard for him to understand our problems. He is like a nuclear physicist becoming frustrated with a child who cannot subtract apples. Bill Gouldd has gone into a city where he knows no one and cranked over $300,000 in volume in three weeks. I come to him complaining that $5,000 a month in personal volume is a lot. He thinks I'm an idiot.

Mr. Gouldd and I have distinct personalities. We see things from different perspectives. Sometimes we clash. Actually it's never much of a clash. I say something, he yells at me, and then I don't say anything back. I hold the record for being yelled at on conference calls. I'm one of the few who speak up. Other people ask me privately, "Why do you even bother to say anything? You know he's just going to yell at you."

When I first started, Mr. Gouldd said something I later took to heart, "It's better to say something stupid, get yelled at, and learn, than not say anything and stay scared, spineless, and stupid." I figure his way of seeing the world is so unlike mine that I can learn by seeing the situation from his perspective. I wish that he would see mine. I seriously begin to question whether I'm in the right company, if I've found my home.

I'm reading *Zen and the Art of Motorcycle Maintenance*. I'm as confused as Phaedrus. I zealously motivate others to follow a path I question. One line jumps off the page: "When people are fanatically dedicated to political or religious faiths or any other kind of dogmas or goals, it's always because these dogmas and goals are in doubt."

Doubt. The thought I try hardest to avoid keeps demanding attention. Rather than looking at the core issues, which are creating my ambivalence, I struggle to retrieve the passion I once had for the business. I work harder. I'm physically tired and emotionally drained—insincerity is exhausting. The more I try, the less I do. People can sense I'm not speaking my truth, so naturally, they don't listen.

Rafael is working in Anaheim. We have a spare bedroom, so he moves in with "the family" for a few months. We've been through a lot over the years.

I get home from the office late one day; Rafael's stuff is gone. No note, just gone. There's a big seminar this weekend, so I figure I'll see him there. He doesn't come. Rumors start. I'm questioned. "Did Rafael leave the company?" At first I laugh, but more and more people ask. I start to wonder. None of the Spanish market is at the seminar. I just talked with him three days ago. He was living in my house for months, living with my family. If he were going to leave, I'd know.

I find out he'd been planning the exodus for months. He had signed up with Enrich International—a multilevel company with a similar product line to Equinox. He informed his key leaders, telling them to keep quiet. One week before the event, he quietly told the Spanish market about a huge meeting in Monterey, Mexico. Adding to the excitement, he said the meeting was just for special, hand-selected people.

Rafael told them "the company" would finally be in Mexico. He neglected to tell them which company. They had assumed Equinox, so when he told them Enrich, many were shocked and some were angry. But of the one thousand people at the meeting, about eight hundred signed with Rafael. Most of the rest got confused and quit.

The month before, Rafael's group had produced over $800,000 in sales volume with Equinox. Now that volume and my security have left. It's a shock. I'm catatonic for three days. He'd become such a part of my life; I'd stopped appreciating him, stopped seeing his needs. In some ways it was like a bad marriage—I received more than I gave. I read once that inequity cannot endure.

I've lost my strongest leg.

The first shock is financial, but what eats at me is the emotional part. We were friends. We had a six-year relationship. He was living in my home with my family, and he just left! Plus, I hear that he slandered me at the meeting. Two weeks later he calls.

"Rob, I couldn't tell you. You might have tried to influence people to stay."

"Why did you leave?"

"Because Equinox is never fucking going into Mexico."

"Rafael, you know they're planning to be in Mexico in four months."

"They've been saying that for over a year, Rob. I talked to Steve Gould." He's the president of Equinox and Bill Gouldd's brother. "I asked him directly and he told me, 'I don't want to hear anything about Mexico. Forget Mexico.' That's a direct quote. I couldn't keep my people waiting forever. I had to make a decision."

"Was that the only reason?"

"Did you read that trainer's contract they want us to sign?"

"No, I just signed it."

"You should've read it, man. It controls you for the rest of your life. There was no way I was going to sign that contract. It's bullshit."

"I didn't even read it. Maybe I'm too trusting. But, Rafael, why did you slander me?"

"Rob, I didn't say one bad thing about you. I taped the whole thing because I knew rumors like this were going to start."

"Then why did five separate people who were there call me and say you did?"

"I don't know. Ask them."

"Whatever. Listen, I hope you do well. I'm sorry to lose you. Do you think you'll come back when Equinox goes to Mexico?"

"I don't know."

"I know Mr. Gouldd wants to talk with you. Why don't we get on a three-way call?"

"Rob, I don't want to get yelled at."

"No, he's not pissed. He just wants to talk."

The three of us talk. I'm impressed. Mr. Gouldd gives Rafael his blessing. "Rafael, we let you down. We said we'd be in Mexico twelve months ago. You had to make a call to preserve your sales force. I would've done the same thing. I hope we might work together in the future."

Wow. Normally, once someone changes jerseys, he's the enemy. Mr. Gouldd always says the best defense is a strong offense. If someone leaves the team, crucify him to preserve the integrity and loyalty of the other players. Instead, he handles the situation with class. He sees Rafael's position.

I'm glad nobody hates anyone, but I've still lost most of my income. What would Mr. Gouldd do? He'd go to work, build it back. He'd get pissed. I get re-motivated. I work with a new passion; some might call it desperation. I'm not asking anymore. I'm leading, and people are following. That next month I get a check for over $26,000—without Rafael. It's a good feeling.

For six months I've been getting mailings from Jay Abraham, a self-proclaimed marketing genius. His credentials are impressive. He's giving a seminar in Los Angeles, $5,000 for three days, one hundred percent money back guarantee, plus I can keep all the written information for investing my time. I decide, with Rafael gone, my business needs a boost. *What do I have to lose?* For the $5,000 fee, I get to bring one person free. I bring Khristina.

Where Bill Gouldd is intimidating, Jay is empowering. I learn a new model of leadership. People ask stupid questions and he doesn't rip their heads off; he's cordial. He starts the seminar on time and is respectful of each person in the room. There are about five hundred people, half of whom paid the $5,000. The other half are their guests. Jay is making serious money, but the information is worth it. Nobody asks for their money back.

I learn about how more money can be made on the "back-end" than the initial sale. I acquire techniques about test marketing, mailings, direct response advertising, and joint ventures. My atrophied creativity is awakening. I love ideas and finding new ways to solve old problems. Mr. Gouldd teaches us not to think, to just follow the system. By repeatedly being called a "fucking idiot" whenever I offer new ideas on conference calls, my creative juices have become a polluted trickle.

Ideas are flowing from Jay's seminar, but I start to realize I won't be allowed to implement them. We aren't supposed to do mailings or telemarketing or joint ventures. We cannot use Equinox's name in any self-produced literature. I will be blackballed if I attempt to do anything outside of "the system."

With Equinox and Advanced Marketing Seminars, Bill Gouldd controls the back-end exclusively: the audio tapes, videos, T-shirts, brochures, and especially the trainings. Bill Gouldd does the big trainings personally, but the "Basics" are taught by a hand-selected group of top producers. I've been honored to be part of this group. The experience is incredible, but the financial compensation is minimal.

I'm an assistant trainer for a seminar in the Midwest. There are two trainers for each "Basics." Advanced Marketing Seminars collects over $250,000 for the weekend; for my efforts I'm paid $1,500. None of us complain, because we know we'd be yelled at and replaced. There are hundreds of people who would gladly do the trainings for free.

There's another "Journey." The price has gone up. It's now $2,500 for the week. About one thousand people attend. Bill Gouldd doesn't want the leadership there. He says people are intimidated when we're sitting in their group. I pay for Khristina to go.

During the week I get three calls from friends saying that Bill Gouldd is hitting on my girlfriend. There's a rule at "Journey" that nobody can have sex during the week of the seminar. It's supposed to be a safe place where people can be open and vulnerable. Even husbands and wives are supposed to refrain. And here the leader, the man on stage, the person everybody paid to see, is trying to break his own rule with my girlfriend.

I decide to talk to Khristina personally before jumping to any conclusions. She's ecstatic about the week and her personal growth. I have to ask, "Khristina, three people called me and said Mr. Gouldd was hitting on you."

She looks down at the ground. "He was flirting."

"Define flirting."

"Well, just each time he would come by my table, he would whisper some little joke or something in my ear."

"And you were enjoying it."

"Well, it was flattering."

"Did anything else happen?"

"If you're asking if we slept together, the answer is no. But his flirting got more graphic." She looks at the ground again.

"Keep going."

"Well, when we were all at the pool, he called me over to his lounge chair. When I got there he said, 'I bet about twelve guys just had an orgasm in the pool watching you walk over here in that bikini.' "

"And what did you say?"

"Nothing."

"Ah, come on, you were flirting back."

"Well, it was flattering." She starts to get defensive. "Out of all the women there, he picked me. It felt good. I got to spend so much personal time with him. He tied my string to his lounge chair so I couldn't leave. We talked for over an hour." At "Journey," a string is tied to each person's wrist as a symbol of the past.

"So you just talked."

"Yeah, but he wants to fly me out to visit him in Florida."

"Are you going?"

"I don't know. I'm confused. I care so much about you, but he's Bill Gouldd. What if it could work? What if I'm the one for him?"

"You really think he's thinking about a long-term relationship? He just wants one thing, Khristina."

"Maybe you're right. All I know is I've never felt as important as when I was sitting by his lounge chair. Everybody was looking at me. Everybody wanted to be where I was."

It bothers me. I pay Howie to clear the emotional triggers that are making me react. I try not to fire my petty jealousies, to make myself see the bigger picture.

I think of my parents. My mom and dad were at a Carl Rogers Encounter Group when my mom first met Doug. They were both immediately attracted to each other. My mom, confused by her feelings, told Dad. Instead of being jealous, instead of reacting, Dad invited Doug to our house the next weekend. Anybody his wife had such an immediate response to had to be special, and he did not want to deny her or himself that friendship. Doug became a best friend of both my parents. It was one of my father's finest moments. Eight years later, when Dad died, his last wish was that my mom would marry Doug.

For the last fifteen years my mom and Doug have shared an incredible romance. What if my dad had been the typical reactionary, jealous male? My mom would've never known her future husband. Yet for some reason, I don't think Mr. Gouldd's intentions are quite as noble.

His assistant keeps calling Khristina, asking her to fly out. Bill Gouldd has done this before with other top producers' significant others. The Alpha dog proving his dominance. I remember his words at the Ranch: "Don't piss me off. I could get any one of you kicked out at any time." I don't confront him. The fear and my weakness gnaw on me. I lose self-respect. Khristina and I break up.

I'm confused. I'm not passionate about the business. The only thing I enjoy is the trainings. I feel I have something to contribute.

I'm on a flight back from a "Basics" in the Midwest. I'm sitting next to one of the top seven money earners in the company. His checks dwarf mine. I hope to pick his brain, find out what he does better than I do. "What's your secret? How come you make so much more money than I do? What do you do differently?"

He leans toward me and says in a low voice, "I'll tell you what my sponsor taught me: 'Keep'em broke.' "

"What?" I'm confused.

"Keep 'em broke. If your people have money in the bank, they get lazy; they don't work as hard. If you continually encourage your people to buy things they can't afford, they will work harder to cover the payments, and your checks will go up."

I don't like his advice.

The end never justifies the meanness.
Abraham Lincoln

Chapter 15

I don't know for sure how other people are inside—all different and all alike at the same time. . . . I do know how I will squirm and wriggle to avoid a hurtful truth, and when finally there is no choice, will put it off, hoping it will go away.

John Steinbeck

I wake up on November 1, 1995, with a strong desire to buy a house. I've never given much thought to buying a house before, but now it seems like the answer. It'll provide roots, stability. I need something permanent in my life. I start looking. I find a house that fits my needs, but I'm not overly excited. I make an offer and drive down to my folks to show them the pictures and get their advice. "If you're not excited about it, don't buy it," they say.

I'm driving home on Interstate 15 and see a sign for Fallbrook. I've never been there, but I've heard it's nice. I turn off almost without thinking. I see a real estate office and right on the front door is a big picture of my house. I get a chill up my body. I know it's my house.

The real estate agent and I drive to see it. I try to contain my excitement. I'm going to have to negotiate a good price. If I designed a house, this would be it: Santa Fe style, 3,500 square feet, open-beam ceilings, five acres of land on top of a hill with views in all directions. I'm in a daze as I walk around. The agent keeps talking, and I ask to be left alone. This is my house.

Doug and my mom come to see it. Doug is excited. Doug doesn't often get excited about material things. My offer is accepted.

Then I go to my broker to get the loan. "No way. No lender in the country will give you a jumbo loan with your credit. This house is out of your range."

"What do I have to do to make it happen?" I say calmly. I know this is my house.

"You'd have to come up with about $60,000 down in the next two months."

"Done."

"Do you have that kind of money?"

"I will."

I'm passionate again. I've no money in the bank but I start building up my checks. In two months I save $30,000. I'm able to borrow the rest from friends and relatives.

I have the down payment but no loan approval. After my offer on the house is accepted, a higher offer comes in. The owner has to honor my offer for another three weeks, but if I can't get loan approval, I lose the house. I'm not worried. I know it's my house. On the last day, at four-thirty, my broker calls. The loan comes through.

I walk silently around the house, touching the beams, running my hands along the counter, slowly realizing I own it.

One week after I move in, I'm unpacking and find the blue goal card I wrote in 1990. The card says, *I enjoy the tranquillity, peace, and power I feel from purchasing my 3,000-square-foot, Santa Fe style home on five acres of land in November 1995.* I sit on the floor of the garage, dazed. I have received exactly what I'd asked for, on the date I'd asked for it five years earlier. Even though I'd forgotten, my subconscious hadn't. Bill Gouldd teaches some amazing stuff.

It's a magical house. There are fifty miles of horse and running trails that twist through the hills, and two beautiful streams that flow year-round. I begin to run again. I begin to enjoy. It's a happy, peaceful time I spend alone. I work little if at all, just enough to qualify for my check.

We have the first official corporate meeting about going into Mexico. Everybody is excited. People keep telling me I'm going to be a millionaire. I see problems. The Mexican economy is the worst it's been in decades. Several large network marketing companies have recently pulled out of Mexico. The products are going to be the same price as in the U.S., but fifteen percent shipping and fifteen percent tax will be added to the cost. Obviously Equinox can't do anything about the tax—that goes to the Mexican government—but fifteen percent shipping? On a $5,000 order, that's $750 to ship a few boxes.

I tell Steve Gould, the President of Equinox, "I could buy a round-trip plane ticket from Mexico City to Vegas, pick up my product, then fly to Hawaii and back for a short vacation, and spend less money than we're charging to have four medium-sized boxes shipped to Mexico." He doesn't appreciate my analogy. I'm not excited about the prospect of working in Mexico.

As I expected, Mexico produces little to no volume. Steve Gould is frustrated because none of the leadership has gone down to help. I decide to leave my sanctuary.

I make a quick trip to Mexico to do a training and assess the situation. It's a nightmare. The leaseholder, Ramon, runs the office like his fiefdom. He has a glassed-in, private suite while everybody else shares small desks. He begins the briefings by saying how incredible he is, how much money he's made, and how he wants to give back to the little people and help them succeed.

He intimidates most of the people in the office. I call an association meeting, and he's voted out. Even though his name is on the lease, he has to go. He's not a bad guy. He's just used to doing business a different way. Oscar Gurria takes over the lease.

I fly back to the U.S. feeling like I helped accomplish something necessary. Three weeks later I move to Mexico City. There are about a hundred people in the room at my first briefing. I'm just finishing when six government agents with guns charge in and arrest me. Victor Pando, always thinking, takes my Rolex and my rings before they haul me and another gringo off to jail in an armored car. Welcome to Mexico.

Several of the associates follow us to the jail to make sure we're all right. My only concern is that last week the U.S. Border Patrol was videotaped beating a family trying to cross into the land of freedom. Mexicans are understandably angry. I hope they don't decide to take revenge.

The guards are friendly but nobody will answer my question of why we were arrested. I am not pleased about having the dubious honor of being the only person in Equinox's history to be arrested while doing a briefing. I call the U.S. Embassy, which is less than helpful, and then order pizza for everyone. I figure if I'm going to be in jail, I might as well make sure the guards like me.

Victor calls Equinox with his cell phone. Fortunate for me, Equinox sends down its lawyer, who is helpful. But it is Patricia Juarez, a person who just signed up in my group, who has the political connections to get us out. She did her $5,000 order in the morning and gets me out of jail that evening. That's a good distributor.

The *capitan* at the jail says I filled out a tourist visa on the plane instead of a work visa. Since I'm doing business in Mexico, I have to pay a fine, fly back to the States, then fly back to Mexico and fill out the right form at the Mexican airport.

"Excuse me, *Capitan*, with all due respect, why can't I just pay the fine and fill out the form at the Mexican airport without flying back to the States?"

"No, you have to pay the fine and fly back to the States and then fly back to Mexico."

We go back and forth. It's a losing battle. Bureaucracy. Through some political contacts, I find out the real story.

The agents who arrested us are the Mexican equivalent of our DEA (I thought they were too well-armed for the wrong-form-filling-out police.) Apparently, Ramon has been angry that he was kicked out of the office and blames me. He informed the authorities that some of the other gringos in the office and I were dealing in drugs. When it became obvious we were not part of the drug cartel, they couldn't just send us away and say "Oops," so they made an issue of the form.

There are some wonderful people in Mexico, and it tears me apart to watch them struggle. I become friends with Victor, Adrian, Liz, Oscar, and many others in the office. I know that the business won't work with the current marketing plan. The average worker makes $3 a day. The average engineer makes $6,000 a year. And Equinox expects them to give $6,500 with tax and shipping to become a manager and then to sell that much each month to qualify for all their bonuses. Almost nobody qualifies for their check.

I also have to sell $5,000 of product every month to qualify. Each month repeats the same nightmare. It's the close of the month. We all need to get qualified. Most of us end up closing a few people using "excess volume." It begins to disgust me.

In the U.S., I can justify the practice because people have a chance to succeed. But in Mexico, I know I'm leading lambs to slaughter. There's no way they will make consistent money with this marketing plan. I keep hoping Equinox will change the plan the next month, then the next, then the next.

Mexicans have a different culture. The family is more important than the peso. They have a balanced life. Most Latinos won't work eighteen hours a day, seven days a week, and that's what I feel it takes to make this marketing plan profitable. It's a full-time plan in a laid-back culture.

I'm living in Mexico City in a two-bedroom apartment with Oscar Gurria—my home sits empty in Fallbrook. Oscar's a great guy who sees a UFO behind every odd light in the sky.

"Oscar, that's Venus."

"Rob, I know it looks like a planet. They do that on purpose to fool us. But if you stare at it long enough in the telescope, you'll see it move."

Victor lives downstairs. He's the most dedicated Equinox person I know. Victor would wear Equinox underwear if they made it. He usually has a phone on each ear talking to two prospects at once and listening to a Bill Gouldd tape at the same time. I've never seen somebody work so hard and make so little.

I decide we need a bonding trip outside the office, a rafting trip down the Rio Filibobos. It's a good excuse to get out of the office. Kelby flies down for two weeks to go with us. We have a great time. I see another dimension of Kelby. He's a wonderful travel partner. It's only a four-day trip, but what an adventure.

The first night we spend in a small colonial village. I've never seen rain so thick. The central plaza is laid with slippery-when-wet tiles, and Kelby is dying to go play in the rain. At first we're cautious, but soon we're hydroplaning on our feet, butts, and chests across an inch of water on the slippery tile. It's quite a spectacle. The residents start to gather and giggle as we laugh and fall. They love it when we fall. Kelby slips and whacks the back of his head on the hard tile. I'm concerned, but Kelby's having way too much fun to feel pain.

The rafting is exciting and inspiring. Kelby's initial fear of the water is quickly gone. We stop every hour or so and explore hidden pyramids and ruins. This is what life's about, enjoying friends and family in the wonders of nature.

On the way home we see a huge crane with people bungee jumping. I've never been bungee jumping. This will be great.

I look down as the crane lifts me. It's scarier than parachuting. When you look down at the ground before jumping out of a plane, the ground is so far below that the fear doesn't register. You don't see death rushing up at you as soon as you jump. The crane is only about eight stories high. My rational mind is screaming, *This is not an intelligent decision.* I jump. One part of me is having fun; the other part is in panic. I'm flying head first at the ground, closer, closer. I feel the tension on the cord and then I'm slung laughing back up in the air.

I'm taking off my harnesses when Kelby comes racing up to me. "Daddy, I want to do it. I want to jump. Please."

"Kelby, it's really scary. Are you sure?"

"Yes, Daddy. Please, please!"

"Why don't we do this: You can go up in the crane with me when Victor jumps. When you see how high you are, then you can decide." I know he's not going to want to jump when he looks down.

We get up to the top. Kelby looks down. "Okay, I want to jump."

I look over at the instructor. He says, "Most children are scared because they mirror the fears of their parents. It's our responsibility to assure that each successive generation lives with less and less fear." This makes me think of my father. The instructor continues, "That's why I do this. To help people over their fear."

I'm not sure if he's sincere or just selling me another ticket. He sounds more like Yoda than Tommy Hopkins; I let Kelby jump.

He's strapped to the instructor for safety and they jump together. He's too light and too little to jump alone. I'm amazed. He's not scared at all. He laughs the whole way and then begs to go again. This time he jumps with me. I'm more scared than he is. At six, Kelby becomes the youngest person to bungee jump in Mexico.

Monday morning, I'm back at the office and Kelby is in summer school. For these two weeks, I work in the morning and play with him in the afternoon. His joy erases my concerns at the office. We have a great time. He becomes friends with Victor, Liz, and Oscar—especially Oscar.

Kelby's trip is a short and needed distraction from a situation I don't know how to solve. Should I leave Mexico with so many people depending on me, or should I keep leading people down a path I question?

I live in denial as long as I can and then start "buying my check." Each month I put in $1,000 to $2,000 to qualify for my bonuses. I continue to ask Equinox to adjust the plan. Steve Gould's response is not encouraging, "We'll look into it." They've been doing that for over a year. "We have a lot of plans for Mexico, Rob, but as a company, we cannot invest any more money until we see some more volume produced."

"Steve, if Equinox will adjust the marketing plan, we'll produce the volume. It's not going to happen the other way around." Apparently this makes sense only to me.

"If you would just forget about the damn marketing plan and produce some volume down there, we could be a lot more flexible. You're so focused on why it's not working, you're not doing what it takes to make it work."

Maybe he's right. Is the volume low in Mexico because the marketing plan needs adjustment or because I need adjustment? I'm looked on as the "leader" in Mexico. It's like a general yelling, "Charge! . . . I think. No, wait, do we have the right gear? Hold on, we might get slaughtered. No, okay. Go ahead . . . charge."

I try, but when I'm not congruent, it's obvious. I don't want to let down the company or my sales force. Again, I'm trying to please others. Sometimes it works. This time it doesn't. The company suffers, my sales force suffers, and I suffer—silently.

Steve Gould has more important disasters to worry about than Mexico. The television program *20/20* does a negative exposé on Equinox. They show Bill Gouldd at a seminar cussing out a lady who dared to make a comment. They interview people who've lost their homes. They basically portray Equinox as a pyramid scam run by a cult leader.

I have a tough conversation with Liz. She's an extremely talented, beautiful young lady who has become a friend. She started with $5,000 and then slowly pulled away from the business. "Rob, I signed up so many people, and none of them are doing Equinox anymore. None of them made any money. Is anybody in Mexico besides you making money?" I find myself saying words I no longer believe. They re-motivate Liz, but not me.

I'm invited to a spiritual seminar. I go, trying to find something. This guy, dressed in tennis shoes, jeans, and a blazer that don't match, starts talking about network marketing, Amway. I roll my eyes. I can't believe they promoted an Amway meeting as a spiritual workshop.

I'm getting ready to leave when he starts talking about spiritual stuff. I like what he says. He's funny, to the point, and brutally honest. I can use some honesty.

His name is Suryavan Xohlar. I love his story. He grew up in Chile and studied with his spiritual teacher in the Andes before becoming enlightened. Some of his students delicately asked, "Your philosophies sound great on the mountaintop, but how do we know they will work in the world we live in every day? Will they solve the problems we have?"

"What's the biggest problem you have?" he replied.

"Money."

"So if I could show you how to make money, that would be a valuable lesson for you." They all agreed. "I will show you how to earn money spiritually and in the process will acquire the necessary funds to buy and protect the mountain, Condor Blanco." Condor Blanco is a sacred mountain he'd wanted to buy to protect it from logging and to use as the center for his spiritual school.

He cut his hair, bought a suit, moved to Santiago, and signed up with Amway. The man then broke the world record with Amway and became a Diamond in seven months.

I'm intrigued. At the break, I wait my turn to speak with him. I'm not sure how to address him. Should I call him the enlightened one? Your holiness? I decide on a more traditional approach. "Sir, I enjoyed what you had to say." He looks at me with deep brown eyes. I stammer, "I . . . I'm in network marketing, also."

"Really, what company?" he responds with a friendly tone.

"Equinox International."

"Ah, yes. I've heard about them. Very interesting. What position are you?"

"International Marketing Director."

"Interesting."

"How did you break the record in Amway, sir?"

"I became who I needed to be to draw the necessary people to complete my goal. Then I worked with each one, individually and spiritually, to help them reach their goal. By helping each individual reach his desire, I attained mine."

I go back to my seat next to Pepe, an eighteen-year-old, highly sexed kid who works in the office. Suryavan's daughter Sol gets up to speak. Sol means "sun" in Spanish. She's beautiful. Pepe looks over at me and whispers in Spanish, "If she's the sun, I'm the moon and I want to have an eclipse." She's extremely well-spoken and confident for her age. She's only sixteen.

After the talk, there's vegetarian food, children enact plays, and we dance. It's a great day. I talk to Sol for a long time. Her eyes are even more mysterious and dark than her father's. She explains to me about the school and the teachings. Every year the school has a month-long retreat at the mountain range they purchased in Chile, Condor Blanco. I decide to go and bring Kelby. Another father-son adventure. The trip isn't until January. Kelby and I will stay for three weeks.

I leave Sol and smile as Pepe walks over to talk with her. I chuckle again about the eclipse comment. We begin doing various exercises to get everybody to mingle. I see a woman I am drawn to. She's standing with her hands in her pockets, looking straight ahead, smiling. I stand closer. She looks straight ahead. She's attractive and unique, exotic. She has an athletic stance. I stand closer. She turns.

We have a nice, brief conversation and she accepts my invitation to dinner. Kimi's intelligent, independent, and spiritual. She fills a void created through my struggles with Equinox. We both get sucked in.

She starts in the business and invests $5,000. She's excited and has great contacts. Maybe this is what I need to get re-motivated. I sponsor a top quality guy beneath her, Jaime Sanchez Montemayor. He used to be the president of one of the largest banks in Mexico. I really like him. He also comes in for $5,000. Maybe I can make this thing work. With the right people, who knows?

Kimi comes to the States and meets my parents and Kelby. They all think she's wonderful, and so do I. She moves in with Oscar and me. I begin to pull away. Now I know how Val felt. The more Kimi tries to please me, the more I pull away. I don't know why. She's being wonderful, but it starts to bug me. She's trying too hard. I don't understand, but I'm becoming annoyed. My mom always taught me, "You can't explain feelings. They just are."

I decide I need to be alone. Kimi doesn't take this news well. I've never had a bad break-up. I'm best friends with both my ex-wives. Seana calls me her "wasband." I think it's cute. I get along with each of my ex-girlfriends. But Kimi's different. She's angry. When she walks in the room and I'm there, the temperature drops fifteen degrees. When I'm doing the briefing, she glares at me. People start to comment about her energy in the office.

When the personal relationship ends, so does the business relationship.

It becomes difficult to work side by side. Mr. Gouldd warns about this. Of course, he puts it delicately: "Don't fuck your money."

It's awkward because Kimi doesn't have anyplace else to live, so she's still living with Oscar and me. I always end up in these weird living arrangements.

Finally, I've had enough and I confront her. "Look, you can live here till you find a place. But you can't glare at me like I'm a piece of garbage. And please say 'hello' or 'how are you' when I say 'hello.' Don't just ignore me in my home." She walks out the door without saying a word.

I can understand her anger. She fills a need in me and then she's no longer needed.

For an unholy relationship is based on differences, where each one thinks the other has what he has not. They come together, each to complete himself and rob the other. They stay until they think there is nothing left to steal, and then move on. And so they wander through a world of strangers, unlike themselves, living with their bodies perhaps under a common roof that shelters neither; in the same room yet a world apart.

From A Course in Miracles

Chapter 16

*To see a world in a grain of sand
And heaven in a wildflower
To hold infinity in the palm of your hand
And eternity in an hour*

William Blake

Finally it's January, and Kelby and I get to spend three weeks together in the Andes of Chile. No offices, no ad calls, no briefings, no Equinox.

It's a long trip involving several planes and buses. Kelby's a great traveler. The camp is nestled in a valley by a swiftly flowing river. We set up our tent under a tree. Kelby starts playing with the other kids, and I go for a long run in the mountains. I'm away from everything and begin to reconnect with what matters.

The camp has about three hundred people from all over Latin America. Kelby and I are the only people from the U.S. Everybody sleeps in tents. A large communal kitchen serves three hearty vegetarian meals a day. In the morning, we greet the day with yoga, deep breathing, and aerobics. After breakfast, we all get in a big circle and Suryavan talks about the energy of this day and shares a spiritual lesson. Even the children listen attentively.

The instructors talk about their courses and then we each choose a three-day workshop. The river looks great, so I choose rafting. Jamba is my instructor. He leads us through a series of exercises to help us "understand the river" and our "ability to work with the natural flow and energy of water."

We are standing on the riverbank. His words are slow and powerful. "Look at the river. Where the water flows, it is pure, clear, and light. Where the flow is restricted or blocked, the water becomes fetid, murky, and dark. Our lives work the same. When we block the flow, problems fester. When we bring light and love to any situation, the natural flow is restored. The problem becomes but a memory from which we learn. In our modern society we are separated from the flow. We forget what makes us whole and holy.

"Go to the river and pick up a rock, a special rock, the rock that holds all of your problems." I reach in and grab a medium-sized rock. Jamba continues, "None of you stepped in the water. You all just reached in from the bank. Is that how you handle your problems? Do you try to avoid any contact with them? Ignore them? Do you just keep doing what you did to create the problem, expecting it to solve itself?" *Whoa, he got me there.*

"Go into the water, and solve your problem." We're fully dressed. Some people start to remove their shoes. "You don't have time to take your shoes off. Your problem is right there. Go solve it now." His voice becomes more forceful.

The water is cold, and the rocks are slippery. I reach under and pick up a rock that feels right and go back to the bank. "Now look at your rock. Is there a difference from one side to the other? Carlos, is there a difference?"

"Yes, the bottom side is clean and the top is slippery and mossy."

"That is usually the way it is with problems," Jamba continues. "On the surface, they look worse than they are. If you turn them over and look from a different angle, the solution is usually obvious." *That's a great analogy.*

"Now, some of you picked large rocks and some of you picked little rocks. Ask yourself, your inner guide, is the rock the size of your problem, or the size of your confidence in your ability to deal with the problem?" I picked a good-sized rock, but the problem seems bigger.

"Now put all of the energy of the problem into the rock, concentrate. When you feel you're ready, not before, throw the rock and your problem back in the river, back in the flow. Throw it with all the energy you have."

I'm concentrating. Putting Equinox, the marketing plan, my confused feelings, all of the turmoil onto this rock. I hear other rocks splash into the water. Some people yell as they throw, others are crying. I'm standing straight up concentrating on my rock. I hear Jamba in my ear:

"You think too much—no problem is solved by simply thinking. If you hold that problem much longer, it will become a part of you. Action solves problems."

I throw my rock with all my energy and let out a yell. My eyes are still closed. I hear Jamba laughingly say in my ear, "I'm not sure if you're just holding back or if you really don't know who you are. Get another rock."

I get my next rock and take deep breaths, focusing all of my energy on this rock, all of my problems. After ten increasingly powerful breaths, I throw the rock with intensity, strength, and a powerful yell.

Jamba again whispers in my ear, "You're holding back. Why? What are you afraid of?"

I hate being told I'm not giving all my effort, especially when I am.

I get another rock. I begin to get angry. "Good, you're mad. At least that is a genuine emotion." This makes me even madder. I throw the rock with such force that I fall in the river. "Good! You have to get into a problem in order to solve it, not run away from it like you've been doing."

How does he know that?

"Keep going, Rob, you've just started. Why are you afraid of letting go, afraid of losing control? Sometimes by giving up control, we gain freedom."

I stop and think about that. *Give up control to gain freedom. That makes sense.* "Roberto, stop thinking and start acting."

I jump waist deep in the river and start throwing rock after rock. I'm completely soaked in the frigid water, but I'm warm. My eyes are closed. As soon as I release one rock, I grab another. An image of my father flashes through my mind. He's smiling at me. I start to cry. I fall in the water sobbing. I had so wanted to please my father, but he had been unhappy with himself and couldn't share approval he didn't have. Oh, he had said the words, "I'm proud of you no matter what you do." But he hadn't shared the actions.

I submerge in the water and let the stream carry me. I release. I let go. There is a physical shift. When I come back, Jamba is smiling at me.

I walk back to my tent thinking, *Why did I wait for a river in Chile to have this breakthrough? Why do I make things more complicated and more dramatic than they need to be?* I understand intellectually what I've just felt, but I have never before experienced the cathartic shift which just occurred. Maybe the difference is somebody pushing me. I am forced to look at what I've tried to avoid.

The next day we ask the river for permission to ride her waters. I'm at the left front position; Gilmer is on the right. Gilmer is athletic and a good person to have on an adventure. The river is more powerful, massive, and exciting than the one in Mexico. We respond quickly to Jamba's commands and negotiate the river without being flipped.

The next day we reflect on what it feels like to work with the flow of the river instead of against it. We share a three-day eco-spiritual adventure. It gives me an idea for a new business venture in the States. I'm beginning to seriously think about leaving Equinox.

A trip is planned to climb Condor Blanco. Since the school purchased the land four years ago, nobody has ever reached the top. It will be a spiritual journey. All of us are in a circle, and Suryavan begins to call out the names of the men who've been selected to go. No women will be on this trip.

Suryavan calls out, "Ivo." Ivo is from Brazil. He is svelte, strong, and one of the most athletic and graceful men I've ever seen.

"Gilmer." Yes, my rowing buddy made it.

"Roberto Styler." Yes, yes, yes. I run to the middle of the circle and join Ivo and Gilmer. The other eleven members join us as their names are called. We all share the honor of being chosen.

I ask Kelby if it's okay for me to go.

"Daddy, I was so happy you got picked. I don't want you to leave me, but you have to go." He's so sweet.

"Do you want me to ask Kimi to stay with you in the tent?" Kimi and I do not have much contact at the camp, but she is still wonderful with Kelby.

"No, Daddy, I want to stay by myself. I'm big enough." Tears fill my eyes as I smile.

The first day is preparation, both physical and spiritual. We work on ropes, knots, and rappelling. We collect our sacred objects, one from each of the four directions. Suryavan talks to us about the power of the vision quest we are about to enter. We will never be the same.

The next day we leave early in the vans. When we get to the gate, we're told to walk in silence. After about forty minutes, Lexvert, who is the instructor for the journey, tells us to look only at the ground directly in front of our feet. We walk like this for another ten minutes. He has us line up in a row facing him, still looking at the ground. He speaks slowly, with power.

"Slowly lift your sight. So slowly that it takes you at least five minutes before you can see the horizon. Slowly lift your eyes and your spirits. What you will see will change your life. Slowly, so slowly you can barely tell your gaze is lifting."

My gaze moves gradually from the dirt at my feet, to the green grass in the field, to the green of the thick jungle, to the two-hundred-foot waterfalls that plunge from the rocky plateau, to the snow, to Condor Blanco! A chill of electricity runs down my body. I'd seen pictures, but never the real thing. Tears fill my eyes.

Lexvert yells, "Now run to the river!" It shocks me. The others are already running ahead, but one thing I can do is run. I reach the river first, breathing deeply.

"Take off all your clothes," yells the assistant instructor, Amiro. All of the instructors use their spiritual names.

We strip and stand naked waiting for the next instruction. "Find a pool deep enough to submerge your entire body. When I say 'now,' put your whole body under the water and do not, I repeat, do not come up until instructed. Do you all understand me? Do not come up until instructed." We all nod. "Now."

The water bites into my skin. It's so cold it burns. I relax. I stop resisting and let the water flow around me. It seems warmer. I remember about the rafting experience and working with the flow of water. I wonder if I can hear him under the water. My lungs start to burn. I begin to think. The water is cold again.

"Now!"

I come up and breathe deeply, refreshed.

Lexvert joins us at the riverbank. "The water that has just surrounded your bodies flowed from the top of Condor Blanco. It has flowed from where we are going. As it naturally flows from high to low, we naturally journey from low to high. Physically and spiritually. We will do many such exercises during this trip, for this is not our egos conquering the mountain, but rather the mountain allowing us to conquer our egos."

Five of us are chosen to clear the trail. The rest stay back at the cabin that was built for Suryavan and divide the food for each pack and prepare the gear. It's dense, thick jungle and slow going. We see our first condors soaring above.

Of the five people, I'm by far the least skilled with a machete. The good news is they give me plenty of room to work. It takes about three hours of intense work to make a narrow trail barely a mile long. Exhausted, we race back to get the others. The cut bamboo stakes protrude out of the steep hillside. Falling would not be fun.

It takes the rest of the day to reach the first camp. We sleep on rock ledges by the side of the stream. We get up early and begin the harder, more technical climbing. The scenery is spectacular. After a few hours we do the naked water ritual again. This time it's under a waterfall. Now the frigid water is also pounding down from an eighty-foot drop. It's exhilarating. We each give a victory whoop.

As we get closer to the summit it looks more and more forbidding. The clouds hide and then expose the sheer rocky peak. As we climb, we chant, asking for permission to climb the mountain. Lexvert explains the importance of our purity: "I have tried to climb this mountain several times. I've never made it to the summit, but I've begun to understand her moods. When our thoughts are clear, the sky is clear. We can see to the summit. If we have doubts or fears, she will cover with clouds and fierce winds. Our purity will determine our success."

It's amazing watching the condors. They're colossal and graceful as they continually circle the summit. The most we see at one time is twenty-two.

There are mountains all around, but the giant birds circle and guard Condor Blanco. For centuries, she has been a sacred ridge.

The terrain now is rocky, but not as steep. Gilmer and I hang back to encourage Claude. His steps are slow, labored, and deliberate. He keeps asking us to leave him, to just go on ahead. But we don't. Most of my life I've been in a leadership position. Here, in the pecking order, I am far down the list. Ivo is the most athletic and takes a natural leadership role. Lexvert and Amiro are the instructors. Darius knows the most about ropes, knots, and climbing. When decisions have to be made, those four talk, and the rest of us follow.

We get to the back side of the summit. Ivo, Darius, and Amiro go off to find the route. I ask Lexvert if I can go, too. He says no. I hate being left out. We sit for about an hour. They come back and say there is no way up from this angle and suggest going around to the left. I think I can see a route between two ridges. They say it's impossible. I'm ignored. We go around the left side and encounter a sheer cliff. We spend another hour on this exploration. I talk to Lexvert again, "I don't know why, but I'm sure I know how to get up. I know the route; just let me try."

"Rob, is it your higher self that is guiding you or your ego wanting to lead?"

That shuts me up for another hour. We're still on the left side but Ivo, Darius, and Amiro have gone back to look for another route. I'm sure I know the way. I tell Lexvert I'm going to find them. He doesn't respond. I don't wait.

When I find them, they're trying a route right next to the one I know is the way. I try to convince them. They're getting annoyed with me. I grab the shoulders of Amiro and look straight in his eyes, "Amiro, I know the way."

He looks at me, then speaks slowly. "I believe you. Go. When you reach the top, come back and show us the route." That's all I need. I move quickly around the ridge before he can change his mind.

I'm awake in a dream. I've seen this route before. I don't know where, but I've seen it. As I climb over a ledge, I know what it's going to look like before I get there. My hands naturally find the best holds, my feet slip into the most secure jams. I'm climbing far beyond my ability. I'm fluid. No fear. It feels natural, like I've done it before, like I'm coming home.

I get to an overhang that's tricky. I'm in a position where I've committed to the point where I can't go back, but I can't move forward either. My legs and arms begin to shake from supporting the weight of my body. I feel fear. The fall would be death. Using my chin as a fifth balance point, I scrape my way up.

I'm too close to the rock to see the peak. I've passed the hardest part. It's a fast climb now and when I reach the top, I'm not sure I've made it. From below, it looks like a sharp point, but it's flat and rocky. I find the highest flat rock and spread my four sacred objects—a rock, a root, a seed, and a flower—in the four directions surrounding me. I sit with my arms stretched wide like the condors and thank the mountain for sharing her gift with me.

I spend only about twenty minutes alone at the top. I should show the others. Just as I'm heading down, Amiro comes over the ridge. He's ecstatic. We high-five and hug powerfully. His whole body exudes joy.

"We did it, Rob, we did it. We're at the top of Condor Blanco. When I looked in your eyes, I was sure you knew the way. You are a special soul, Rob, a special soul."

In an instant, I feel deep joy and love. He is genuinely thrilled that I made it first. No ego. I receive a powerful lesson. It is the first of four the mountain has planned for me.

Amiro asks me to climb back down and show the others. He needs to be alone. On the way down, I run into Ivo on his way up. He's excited we made it and moves gracefully up the rock.

The whole group has already begun to follow the route. They yell in excitement when they hear we reached the top. We spend the next hours laying and securing the ropes for the others to follow.

Darius warns us about the condors that are circling dangerously close. Apparently they "hunt" by ramming their prey off balance and making them fall off the cliffs. I knew condors were scavengers, but I had no idea they played such an active role in creating the carcass. One person stands guard as the other two fasten the ropes.

It's a tedious, time-consuming task. It's now 6 P.M. It won't get dark till 10:30, but we have to start heading back. We'll try again tomorrow. Only three of us have made it to the top. I'm quiet the rest of the day.

We get stranded on the mountain by the night. We feel our way down the cliffs like Braille. It's not a good situation. Amiro and I go ahead to set up the tent and prepare the food.

We are spreading the tarp when we hear screaming. In the blackness, we race toward the noise. A large boulder has fallen and smashed into Gilmer's shoulder. We think it's broken. We all work together to get him down safely. We're not able to reach the first camp and have only one tent for all of us and no sleeping bags. Gilmer sleeps in the middle to be kept warm. I go off on my own under the stars. I cover myself with branches and leaves for warmth. It's a restless sleep, but I feel like I need to be alone. The summit was powerful, but it feels unfinished.

We plan to rest one day and then try again. This time all of us are going to make it. I start thinking about Kelby. I've already been to the top. Instead of spending two more days away from him, I should go back. I ask the team if my leaving would be okay. We talk about it for a long time. What's the big deal? I made it, now it's time for me to go back. At first I'm confused, then I'm touched.

Amiro puts it the clearest: "Rob, I would never tell another human being what he should do. I understand your desire to be with your son. But you're a part of this team. We began this journey together. A team should not be broken. We need you. Whatever you decide, we'll support you. The decision is yours, not ours." I decide to stay. I've learned my second lesson, about ego and team.

In college, I ran cross-country and track—me against every other runner. It feels good to be part of a team. At the beginning, Bill Gouldd gave me a feeling of team. I felt like I was part of a holy crusade to save the planet. Recently I've felt like the little kid who sees the emperor has no clothes. The difference is, where the little boy screamed out, I've said nothing.

We are sitting around the fire eating. I begin to get light-headed, dizzy. An hour later, I'm violently sick. I have to be carried like a baby to my tent. I soil my shorts. I'm helpless. But each person, in his own way, helps me. I learn the third lesson, the lesson of interdependence.

I can't hold in any food. It's only 11 A.M., but I sleep all day. They keep checking on me and chanting prayers. Amiro tells me, "We are spiritual beings. Your spirit has been through a lot. It is adjusting. Give it time."

It starts to rain. The next morning I feel better. We have to hike out because of the weather. Gilmer, whose shoulder was not broken, comes to my tent. "It means a lot to each of us that you decided to stay. We all agreed last night that if you weren't better, none of us was going up without you." My eyes fill with tears.

When we get back, the whole camp is excited. Kelby jumps in my arms. Suryavan congratulates us all. It's an incredible feeling.

That night I know I have to go back, alone. In the morning I talk to Kelby again.

"Kelby, I will only be gone a day and half this time." Traveling alone is much faster. "I have to go back up the mountain."

"Daddy, you just got back."

"I'll be gone much shorter. I know this is our special trip but I have to do this."

"I know," he pauses. "You're not done yet."

I look at my child. He's six years old. How could he know I'm not done yet?

I ask Suryavan for permission. "No way. It is too dangerous. Alone it is impossible." It's strange hearing him say "impossible," but I'm committed.

"I made it to the top by myself without ropes. The ropes are still in place for the next trip. All of the hard parts already have fixed ropes. I know I can do it. It is something I have to do, alone. I brushed across a part of my spirit I've never experienced. I would begin to enter that space and then someone would talk or make a joke, and I would be pulled back out. Plus, the food we ate was processed junk. I want to eat only the plants of the mountain to purify my spirit. It's something I have to do."

"I understand your desire, but it is not fair to the school to let one person risk the future. If something should happen, it is our land. We are responsible. I cannot let you go. What if you get sick again? What if you get hurt, alone?"

I ask again and again. For three days I ask. I write letters asking. I explain why. I ask over and over.

The whole school is taking a bus and then walking to the cabin where we first saw Condor Blanco. I quickly pack for my journey, expecting and preparing for what I want.

At the base of Condor Blanco, nine others and I are initiated into the school. I ask Suryavan again, handing him a signed letter releasing the school from any liability. He smiles, "Your persistence is impressive. I admire your commitment. I have done many things in my life alone. Things only I understood were necessary. Others often thought me strange or insane. Each soul must be true to itself. Go with my blessing."

Yes! Yes! Yes! I grab my pack, kiss Kelby, and head up before Suryavan can change his mind. My pack is light, only my sleeping bag, water bottle, harness, and emergency first aid. I forage along the way and collect dinner from the plants. Every cell in my body tingles.

I do the naked water ritual and continually chant, asking the mountain for permission to climb her. I didn't get started until 3 P.M., but I reach the base camp before six. I make a salad with the plants I collected and then, for two hours, I lie on my back and watch the condors circle above. I imagine what it must feel like, the wind rushing through their feathers, gliding on the thermals, looking across the world.

I sleep deeply and wake up at 4 A.M. It's still dark, but I'm anxious to get started. The climb goes quickly. I reach the bottom of the peak by 10 A.M. Again I feel fluid climbing the sheer rock, but this time the sun has not heated the mountain yet and the rocks feel like ice. My hands begin to get stiff, and my grip weakens. I'm glad the ropes have been laid for security.

I reach the peak. I feel completion, not celebration. I'm alone. I can spend time on the summit. I spread my four sacred objects and sit in the center of the circle. Again I sit with my arms spread wide like the condor, my eyes closed. I see my father and Bill Gouldd, the two men I've most wanted to please, fighting.

A chill of electricity runs up my spine. It is clear—the fourth lesson. I cannot please them; they are not pleased with themselves. I did not need a sacred mountain in Chile to understand this. The mountain simply released what I knew all the time. It could have been a piercing question from a friend, a powerful quote, or simply slowing down long enough to hear my quiet voice say, "Stop. Look. Feel. Are you moving toward or away from your highest vision? Be aware."

I have to smile. What we most desire, we often chase away. I could have had approval from both men, if I'd only been true to who I am.

We sit together, the mountain and I, until only
the mountain remains.

Li Po

Chapter 17

Whenever there is fear, it is because you have not made up your mind. Your mind is therefore split, and your behavior inevitably becomes erratic. . . .This can be corrected only by accepting a unified goal.

A Course in Miracles

Climbing back down, I think how most of us dwell next to our spiritual mountains our whole lives, but the climb is internal. At times we hear a soft voice, "This is not all there is. Your life was meant to be much, much more. Follow your heart. Let go. Risk. Try."

In a park where I run in Mexico City, there are beautiful trails that wind through the mountains, but all of the people walk and jog around a small oval track—beating a dull, repetitive path of agitated circles.

Instead of listening to our souls, we surround ourselves with seductive distractions, drowning out the patient whisper. If we ever do find ourselves alone, we create a million activities: anything to keep from thinking, reflecting, and being quiet. We rarely question our mission—why are we doing what we're doing? If we feel unhappy or unfulfilled, we keep doing what we've been doing, only faster, believing that simply moving guarantees our arrival.

The mountain taught me the opposite. Only by being still, by separating ourselves from our habits, do we recognize the movements swirling around us and see the patterns we have repeated—the agitated circles.

When I get back to the cabin where I started it's about four in the afternoon. Kimi and three other people on horseback are waiting for me. They've been watching me with binoculars for my safety. They give me a horse, and we are off. What a rush racing down the hill on horseback. I'm exhilarated and exhausted. I've been up since 4 A.M.

They go to swim beneath a huge waterfall, and I hitch a ride back to the camp.

Suryavan is excited when he sees me. "You made it, didn't you? You made it to the top."

"Yes."

"Don't speak to anyone today about your experience. You have to give your spirit time to adjust, to expand. Words will only dilute your power. Congratulations."

I find Kelby, eat, and then sleep.

The next day I look for Suryavan. He is walking by himself. I approach him tentatively, not sure what I'm going to say.

"I think I have to do something that will upset and confuse a lot of people." He thinks about what I said. I like when people think before responding.

"Rob, as we grow and leave our old selves behind, we often leave our old situations and relationships."

My main concern is Bill Gouldd. Suryavan knows people in Equinox, and I don't want to say anything to force my hand at this point. "I think the person I'm most worried about will be extremely angry at my decision."

Suryavan thinks about this and then speaks slowly, "Let me share with you a story. When my teacher first came to these mountains, there was a very wise man who everyone went to for advice. He was famous and much respected. But my teacher was also wise and people began to go to him instead. This upset the first sage very much. One day he confronted my teacher calling him a charlatan and fake. He was very angry.

"My teacher was calm and said, 'I have heard you are very wise.' The angry man agreed and felt better.

"My teacher continued, 'Since you are so wise, I would like to ask you a question. If a man is given a gift but he does not accept it, to whom does the gift belong?"

"The angry sage thought about this, happy to have a chance to show his wisdom. 'If the gift is not accepted, it would then belong to the giver.'

"My teacher smiled and said, 'I do not accept your gift.'

"Rob, if this man you are concerned about is angry because you are following your heart, simply do not accept his gift and his anger will be his to deal with alone."

As Kelby and I fly back to Mexico, the reality of my situation begins to weigh on me. What will I do? How will I make money? How will I tell people?

I live in denial for a few more weeks. I recruit my last person in Equinox, Estephan Lemberg. I try to work the business, but I'm simply building my courage to leave.

I go home to the States. My group in the U.S. thinks I'm in Mexico; the people in

Suryavan with Condor Blanco in the background

Mexico know I'm in the States. Val calls me. Over the years she has become a close friend.

"Rob, I know we're not supposed to talk about negative stuff, but I hate what I am doing. There are too many lies. It's all about money. And worst of all, in order to qualify for my check, I am doing things and saying things I don't believe." She says this quickly, like it has been waiting to come out.

"Val, it is getting to me, too. It's like what we always teach: 'You are who you hang around.' I'm not liking who I'm becoming," I say with a sigh.

"I feel dirty and manipulative," Val continues. "I would rather make less money and be happy and have peace in my life than continue to go through the hell I'm living."

"Val, it is such a relief to talk to you about this because it has been my own private hell; now at least I know you're in there with me." We both laugh. It's a wonderful release. We've been holding these feeling in for a long time. There is a code in Equinox: "Don't piss in the stream." If you have a lack thought, or negative energy, go home. The result is that people quietly suffer, alone.

Once I tell Bill Gouldd I want to sell my salesforce, he begins to publicly slander me, ironically saying I am an "egomaniac." He stands on stage in front of hundreds of people, proudly grasping the *Inc.* magazine with his picture on the cover, and yells, "Who the fuck is Rob Styler? I don't see his picture on the cover of *Inc.* magazine. Rob wanted to change the marketing plan. Our marketing plan made us the fastest growing company in America. When companies change the marketing plan, that is a sign of problems—a sign that the company is going down. We are not going to change our marketing plan and it just shows you how stupid Rob Styler is that he would even suggest it."

His actions make me wonder how I blindly followed him for so many years.

Looking for a new future, Val and I contact other companies in network marketing. We are flown all over the country to visit different corporate offices. It is an ego boost. I begin to recognize the value of the training I received during the last seven years. At first, like a battered dog, I am timid. When asked, I cautiously offer ideas and suggestions. But when I realize nobody is going to yell at me, or call me a piece of shit or a fucking idiot, I let loose. Seven years of thwarted creativity is expressed during animated discussions. It feels wonderful to be heard, acknowledged, and appreciated.

Over the following weeks as rumors spread that I am leaving, many of my friends and associates privately call me, desperately wanting to be heard, understood, and not judged. It's cathartic for them and me.

I begin to write my book. It's addictive. All I want to do is type. Sometimes I forget to eat for an entire day. I only pause when I write something that stops me. I stare at the screen reading the words I just wrote, thinking, *Wow, how did I not see that before?*

I'd been so busy trying to get somewhere that I never questioned where

I was going. Until I took the time to be alone on the mountain, I did not recognize the memories that were whipping me relentlessly onward. Like my father and Bill Gouldd, I thought others could fill my void. The last seven years have been well spent. They have proved a necessary and valuable lesson. The only gift I can be lacking is what I have not freely given.

Many of the other leaders in Equinox begin to express their frustration. At the end of July in Vegas, they have a meeting. For the first time a united leadership confronts Bill Gouldd. A heated discussion begins about sexual improprietes. Bill Gouldd is on the defensive.

In the middle of the argument, one of the of the top people quietly raises his hand. Mr. Gouldd acknowledges him, annoyed "What do you want?"

"Excuse me, Mr. Gouldd, but why did you fuck my wife?"

The room goes silent.

His answer is as pathetic as his action, "I had to, she came to me."

The reaction is unified and angry. As in *The Wizard of Oz*, the curtain has been pulled back. Bill Gouldd feels his control slipping away, the spell being broken.

What good will it be for a man if he gains the whole world, yet forfeits his soul?
Matthew 16:26

Epilogue

After I decide to leave Equinox, all I want to do is sell my sales force, be compensated for what I have built, and move on with my life. Equinox has other ideas. Val Miller, Director of Legal Affairs for Equinox International, states in a letter dated May 27, 1997:

"In the event Equinox chooses to approve the proposed sale of your Distributorship, we would only do so with certain stipulations including, but not limited to, the following:

We would require an unequivocal waiver and release of any past claims or any claims resulting from this proposed sale of your Distributorship. We would also require an acknowledgment of full disclosure regarding the status of this Distributorship. This waiver would require your signature as well as the signature of any purchaser;

We would require a signed release acknowledging that you will not participate in any manner in any competitive company conducting business in the direct sales industry, whether in the U.S. or abroad, for a period of not less than one year; and

We would require a signed release acknowledging that you will not use any training, educational, or motivational materials acquired or exposed to through Equinox or Advanced Marketing Seminars in any future business ventures.

If you disagree with any of the terms set forth in this letter, please have your attorney contact our Legal Affairs Department."

I had no idea I would have to get a lawyer to complete a transaction that is clearly permitted in the Equinox Manual. Part 1, Sections S, Paragraph

2 of the Policies and Procedures states, "Equinox may not unduly deny a 'sale' of the Distributorship."

I page Bill Gouldd and ask if we can talk, hombre to hombre, and work this out. I don't want to have to take the next step and hire a lawyer as the letter from Equinox suggests. Mr. Gouldd leaves a cryptic message on my machine saying, "The karmic debt you are creating will come crashing down on you. You will have to pay big time." That doesn't sound friendly.

I fire back an angry letter to Equinox, which basically says, "How dare you try to limit my freedom."

Steve Gould responds on June 3, 1997. He writes an eloquently worded but just as restrictive letter, "It is not unreasonable for Equinox to request that you sign a non-compete agreement, as well as agree to not use any of the proprietary training materials which have been supplied to you by Advanced Marketing Seminars ('AMS')."

Over the last seven years, I've spent over $100,000 to learn the information AMS "supplied" to me. I went to expensive seminars hoping they would help me in the future. Now they want me never to use the information. That's like going to medical school, paying tens of thousands of dollars, dedicating years of your life, and then being told you can only practice medicine in their hospital.

On June 10, 1997, my lawyer responds to Equinox:

"Even if the inherent ambiguities and inconsistencies in the contract documents could be resolved by a court so as to construe the above provisions in favor of Equinox, you should be advised that California courts generally impose a requirement of good faith and fair dealing in a party's exercise of a discretionary power conferred by a contract. It is extremely unlikely that a California court would find good faith and fair dealing by Equinox are present in this instance, particularly in light of the fact that the restrictions on competition proposed by Equinox are in clear violation of California law and are against public policy. Moreover, even if Rob were to acquiesce in signing a non-compete agreement, it would be void in California by virtue of California Business & Professions Code Section 16600."

That is all I want: "good faith and fair dealing." Val Miller, once he sees that I have a good lawyer, calls that same day and agrees to drop the non-compete clause. I phone my parents and we celebrate. I'm going to be able to sell my distributorship and go on with my life. I call Val Miller back to ask what else I have to do to complete the sale. He says I have to disclose more information about my distributorship and promises to call me first thing Monday morning so we can wrap up this sale. This was on June 10.

He never calls. I call and fax Equinox repeatedly with no response. On July 4, a fax is waiting on my machine from the night before. I have been suspended from Equinox.

Before this whole mess started, I was told by Tom Gaskill, the head of Field Compliance for Equinox, that I was the only International Marketing Director not to have a negative letter on file. But now, Bill Gouldd wants me out. He asks all the leaders for "dirt" on me. They offer no response. Equinox then suspends me for recruiting for another network marketing company. When I show that I am not even signed up in another company, they change tactics.

On numerous occasions, Bill Gouldd said he could have any one of us kicked out for any reason. He joked that he could even suspend us for not sending in our monthly retail receipts—we would nervously laugh.

Per the Policies and Procedures of Equinox International, only Mexican citizens can retail products in Mexico. For the last year, living in Mexico, I could only sell products wholesale and train my people. I would have been breaking the policies of Equinox and laws of Mexico to retail products. This logic apparently makes sense only to me.

Once Bill Gouldd and Equinox hear I want to sell my sales force, they want me out, fast—I am suspended for not sending in my retail receipts. I have to smile when I find a quote for my book from Goethe, "None are more hopelessly enslaved than those who falsely believe they are free."

The money for the sale of my distributorship is not worth the frustration. For seven years I have heard about the freedom I was creating and the equity I was building with my sales force. But if I can't sell it, I don't own it.

On Independence Day, 1997, I choose my freedom.

After a while you learn the subtle difference
Between holding a hand and chaining a soul,
And you learn that love doesn't mean leaning
And company doesn't mean security,
And you begin to learn that kisses aren't contracts
And presents aren't promises
And you begin to accept your defeats
With your head up and your eyes open
. . . .
And you learn to build your roads on today
Because tomorrow's ground is too uncertain for plans.
And futures have a way of falling down in mid-flight.
After a while you learn
That even sunshine burns if you get too much.
So you plant your own garden and decorate your own soul,
Instead of waiting for someone to bring you flowers.
And you learn that you really can endure . . .
That you really are strong.
And you really do have worth.
And you learn and learn . . .
With every goodbye you learn.

Veronica A. Shoffstall

The Letter

On September 10, a letter is sent to Bill Gouldd and signed by the majority of the top money earners in Equinox. Here are the main parts:

Dear Bill:

It has been over a month since the Monday (7/28/97) meeting at corporate headquarters with the top money earners of Equinox. That meeting set a precedent. Never before has the leadership confronted you, as founder and CEO, with such strength and unison. Because we refused to be intimidated, we overcame a great fear: standing up to Bill Gouldd. Until Monday you had kept us terrified, using intimidation and fear tactics to keep us cowering and divided. Monday was the day that we discovered that we are unified in our discontent regarding your management tactics. The message we received from you on Monday was that you recognized and acknowledged the extent of the dissension and that from now on you would treat us fairly, as business partners.

As you know, there are many issues that must be resolved. We would first like to restate the issues that were raised on Monday, issues that have been our central concerns for the last several years. None of these issues are new. All have been brought to your attention many, many times in the past and were never resolved.

Issues

We, the distributor force, will no longer accept sexual misconduct. There was not a person in the room on Monday [who] has not had their business suffer because of your transgressions and unacceptable conduct against wives, girlfriends, and, more generally, any good-looking woman in the Equinox sales organization. Both directly and indirectly, all of your leaders have suffered because of your misconduct. Going to trainings so you can pick up women must stop. Advances on our wives and girlfriends must stop. Sexual jokes and offensive conduct to our downline distributors must stop. You are well aware of your misbehavior. You have been confronted many, many times with this issue. We ask that you apologize for past transgressions, cease sexual and insulting misconduct, racially slurred jokes, and the harassment of all women.

Public humiliation and defamation of Equinox leadership and distributors must stop. Addressing personal issues in public must stop. Blatant attacks on leadership to reduce their popularity, credibility, and confidence must stop. . . . Treat people with respect.

Fear tactics must stop.

No more politics. Equinox was promoted as rewarding production; that is why we joined. . . . Your public pronouncements that advancement is determined by whether "I like you" and whether "you are politically acceptable to me" destroy both our morale and our ability to attract and keep quality people.

An independent representative should be able to choose with whom they would like to work. In traditional multilevel companies, distributors have the choice of whether or not they would like to use the founder and CEO as an expert within their sales organization. We do not have that choice. We must pay for and use your trainings. We must pay for and use your videos. We must pay for and use your audio tapes. Not only are we required to use these "optional" sales tools, if we don't vigorously market them to others, it is common knowledge that we will be blackballed from your organization. We must be given independence. Whether or not we use your seminars and materials, or create our own, must be our choice.

You have consistently made deals and then broken them. Agreements must be kept and fulfilled in arrears. The top fifty money earners were pledged a percentage of the (3/29/96) "Perpetual Money Machine" total gate. It was agreed that AMS Senior Trainers, Trainers, and Assistant

Trainers were to be given a percentage of AMS's 1996 Gross Profit. A covenant was reached with Sheri Sharman, Rich Von, Marc Accetta, Greg Ammerman, and Laurie Rubidge guaranteeing them a percentage of AMS's 1997 Gross Revenues. Fulfill your obligations.

Solutions

Open books. Despite repeated protests, no accounting has ever been provided for the debits assessed monthly on our bonus checks. Repeated protests have gone ignored. For almost two years, thousands of dollars have been withheld monthly from each of us. Yet documentation for the deductions has never been provided. We have repeatedly asked for an accounting. We know the debits are inaccurate since whenever the underlying detail was provided, we documented thousands of dollars in miscalculations and always the errors were in your favor. An immediate accounting for all debits must be made available to all representatives with appropriate credits for all insupportable deductions from our accounts.

Many top leaders have vehemently argued with the accounting process related to Equinox's in-house financing contracts, the Courtesy Credit Plans (CCPs). In early '95, John Alden documented significant procedural errors in the way Equinox computes the bonuses paid on CCP contracts. A year-and-a-half later, Equinox returned 41% and 53% of his withheld '93 and '94 bonuses. He was asked to keep the transaction quiet. Why? Why weren't the adjustments implemented company-wide immediately? Every miscalculation must be corrected and credited. An immediate accounting for all CCPs, from '92 to present, must be given to all representatives.

Financial commitments made in the past must be honored and fulfilled in arrears . . . .

Bill, our only intent is to fix our company. We built it, we love what it should stand for, and we are emotionally attached. We want it fixed. In order for the company to ever again prosper, however, we need to forever eradicate the unfulfilled agreements, lies, and ethical and moral transgressions.

Bill, we have repeatedly brought these issues and solutions to the table, requesting action over and over again. The time for Equinox to perform and make good is NOW. We need action: Our issues need to be resolved, our solutions need to be implemented. We sincerely want to fix our company. It can be fixed, but we need your help. Please respond within five working days so that our attorney can formalize this proposal for your attorney's review. It is time!!

Bill Gouldd responds to the letter. On a national satellite broadcast, he suspends the people who signed it for insubordination. They leave to start their own company, Trek Alliance. Bill Gouldd sues nineteen of them for $10 million each. He also files a blanket lawsuit against one thousand "John Doe's" for anyone who tries to recruit an Equinox representative to another multilevel opportunity.

I asked several people who stayed with Equinox if they read the letter written to Bill Gouldd. They said, "No, but Mr. Gouldd told us what it said—they just wanted more money and they wanted to own Equinox. They forgot where they came from and were too greedy."

I used to do the same thing. I lived in denial.

If you can't change your mind, are you sure you still have one?
Bumper sticker

Where are they now?

*Success is always temporary. When all is said and done,
the only thing you'll have left is your character.*

Vince Gill

Kelby

Marina, my first ex-wife, is living in Irvine with her husband, Juan. Kelby is now seven and playing AYSO soccer. Kevin is two and their new baby, Kiany, is a year old.

Bill Gouldd is busy being Bill Gouldd. After publicly saying it is a stupid idea only done by companies that are desperate and failing, Bill Gouldd changes Equinox's marketing plan. He makes weekly conference calls telling people who stayed how the company will be different, and that the departed leaders had forgotten where they came from—all they wanted was more money.

At a seminar in St. Louis, he walks onto the stage holding a gravestone with the images of the top five people who left Equinox. Thousands of people cheer. Again, I am reminded of the line from *Zen and the Art of Motorcycle Maintenance*. "When people are fanatically dedicated to political or religious faiths or any other kind of dogmas or goals, it's always because these dogmas and goals are in doubt."

My original sponsor, Dawn, left four months after I started. She quit right before I began to make money.

Seth, who was my sponsor, drives a snazzy red NSX and recently bought a million-dollar home in Laguna Hills overlooking the ocean. He stayed with Equinox and is now a trainer with Advanced Marketing Seminars. When most of the top people left, there was a vacuum created, and many people who were in the shadows are now in starring roles. I hope, for their sakes, history does not repeat itself.

Casey stayed with Equinox.

Sheri is working hard building a new network, writing a book, and creating a woman's empowerment group. She is also taking time to enjoy playing with dolphins in front of the multi-million-dollar home on the beach she envisioned ten years ago. Over the past months, I have become closer with Sheri than I ever was when we were both in Equinox.

Ironically, on his latest conference calls, Bill Gouldd said that everybody thinks Sheri is a nice person because that is how he marketed her. I think Sheri took the abusive personality of Bill Gouldd and marketed it in a way that made him socially accepted. He had never achieved long-term success before he met Sheri. It will be interesting to see what happens now that Sheri is no longer his buffer. If you want to contact Sheri, she can be reached at 760-942-1990 or www.luvnlife.com.

Joe has a lovely family and a beautiful home on the water with a boat in Florida. We have talked and laughed many times in the past weeks. Like many of us, he wanted to leave Equinox earlier, but financially he could not afford to lose his income. I respect him and his wife Jadee and appreciate their friendship. It is wonderful to see them excited about their new future. If you would like to contact them, they can be reached at (561) 694-9441.

Marc, Joe's friend and a big help to me in the beginning, left the business years ago and now is married with two children. He is in the process of developing a skateboard park to get kids off the street. If you would like to help him create his vision, call (760) 344-2604.

Rafael started his own network marketing company in Mexico: Eco-Mex.

Armando quit two years after starting and before Rafael made big money.

José Lopez died in a car crash in Mexico.

Lori Rubidge is the only founder and top money earner to stay with Equinox.

Rich is a multimillionaire with a wonderful wife and family. He is one of the people who created Trek Alliance. Kale Flagg and Rich actually started forming Trek eight months before they left Equinox. Rich says, "We wanted an insurance policy, a back-up plan. You don't buy fire insurance because you want your house to burn down, but if it burns, you are glad you have it."

Chris, who is famous for the "biscuit" incident, forgot to send in his $25 yearly renewal fee, and from what I heard, it was used as an excuse to kick him out of Equinox. He was making about $15,000 a month at the time. He went to *20/20* and was part of the unflattering exposé of Bill Gouldd and Equinox. True to form, Bill Gouldd is sueing him for millions of dollars.

Seana is still working with Equinox. When all of the top people left, I called to make sure she was okay. She said, "Are you kidding me? I'm excited! I'm one step closer to Bill Gouldd."

Dr. Howie Cohn still has his successful practice and is still working with Equinox.

After leaving Equinox, Val Michels, who has become a best friend and confidant, wrote her mission statement and realized her passion was "to assist others in bringing forth new levels of healing, spirituality, and personal empowerment to their lives." She has formed "The Win/Win Center," home of an online bookstore: WIN/WIN Books & Audios, and WIN/WIN Resources which assists individuals and businesses who wish to develop their mission statements. She also published, "Your Mission Statement Workbook." Val can be reached at winwin@harbornet.com.

Khristina moved back to Florida. I have lost contact with her.

Victor, from what I hear, is doing well in Mexico. I always imagine him with a phone on each ear. I congratulate him. He is succeeding where I did not.

Oscar, I imagine, is still looking for UFOs. I have not heard from him in a few months.

Liz is working hard in Mexico with Equinox and becoming the leader I knew she would. She is a talented woman.

Kimi is in Mexico. I have not heard from her.

Suryavan is expanding his spiritual school into the U.S. and can be reached online at condorbl@chilistat.net.

Sol, the sun, is still making young men swoon.

Pepe, the moon, has a girlfriend.

Rick, my brother, is working with me in our new business, as are my parents who continue their love affair and sage advice.

I am happy and having fun being creative and not being yelled at. Writing this book was a great experience. It made the legal trauma with Equinox bearable. Rather than getting angry about Equinox's legal manipulations, I could laugh with my parents and say, "This will make a great epilogue to the book."

It reminds me of a story I heard about Colonel Sanders. He had just sold Kentucky Fried Chicken and walked into his last board meeting. They were talking about changing the gravy, making it water-based rather than milk-based. The Colonel boomed out, "Don't mess with my gravy!"

The new CEO saw his opportunity to establish authority. "Colonel, we paid you a lot of money, and as it states in the contract, you no longer have any say in corporate decisions. The water-based gravy will save hundreds of thousands of dollars per year and will dramatically increase profits."

Colonel Sanders banged his hands on the table, stood up, and began walking out.

Surprised the Colonel didn't put up more of a fight, the new CEO asked, "Where are you going?"

"Going on the Johnny Carson show. Gonna tell them this shit ain't fit to eat."

Kentucky Fried Chicken still uses milk in its gravy.

Man's capacity for justice makes democracy possible,
but man's inclination to injustice makes democracy necessary.
Reinhold Niebuhr

Disclosure

I altered five events to better fit the story line and changed one name to protect the innocent. 1) The "biscuit incident" happened at a breakfast meeting, not a dinner meeting. 2) My brother told me the story about anger and not accepting the gift, not Suryavan. 3) Joe Locke, Steve Baran, and I never actually swapped ties. I created the story to epitomize fake-it-till-you-make-it. 4) Bill Gouldd made the comment about heterosexual, homosexual, bisexual . . . autosexual, at a later seminar, not when he gave me the hand and body lotion. 5) The gelato scenario with Khristina was altered to make it more entertaining. And George was not the real name of the top producer Bill Gouldd verbally abused on stage. Other than that, to the best of my memory, the story is factual.

Author's Comment

Obviously, though I learned a lot, my experience with Bill Gouldd was less than ideal. I hope this in no way taints anyone's opinion of network marketing. Since I left Equinox, I have become more impressed with the industry and less impressed with Bill Gouldd.

Network marketing is a wonderful industry. Unfortunately, some people exploit it. The only way they can be stopped is if they are exposed. I know writing this book is risky. But if I were to sacrifice my character for temporary security, I would have neither.

On October 29, I spoke with Val Miller, the head of Equinox's legal affairs department. First he told me that Equinox was going to send me a check for $5,800 for past bonuses I am owed from "miscalculations" Equinox made on the courtesy credit plans (over six weeks has passed and I still have not recieved the check). Then he said he heard a rumor that I was going to publish a book and if I did, Equinox would "viciously attack me."

I do not understand the law as well as Val Miller, so I had the book "vetted" by Kirsch and Mitchell, one of the top firms concerning publishing law in the country. They felt the book did not invade Bill Gouldd's privacy and it contains no libel—as long as it is all true (which it is)—but that does not prevent Bill Gouldd or Equinox or anybody from suing me.

Kirsch and Mitchell said, "The sad thing about our legal system is, Rob, that if somebody has big money and they are pissed off, they can destroy your life, legally. Not because they are right, but because they can afford to."

Maybe I am naive, but I believe the first amendment of the Constitution has more power than money. I may be "viciously" attacked in court for writing this book—for telling my truth—but for seven years Mr. Gouldd taught me, "If you don't stand for something, you'll fall for anything. Don't be a puss. Stand up and fight for what you believe."

Thanks, Bill—I learned a lot. I will never again give away my power.

> *Evil will triumph when good people do nothing.*
> Chinese proverb

Our deepest fear is not that we are inadequate. Our deepest fear is that we are powerful beyond measure. It is our light, not our darkness that most frightens us. We ask ourselves. Who am I to be brilliant, gorgeous, talented and fabulous? Actually, who are we not to be? You are a child of God. Your playing small doesn't serve the world. There's nothing enlightened about shrinking so that other people won't feel insecure around you.

We were born to make manifest the glory of God that is within us. It is not just in some of us; it's in everyone. And as we let our own light shine, we unconsciously give other people permission to do the same. As we are liberated from our own fear, our presence automatically liberates others.

Marianne Williamson

If you have comments about this book or would like to contact the author, he can be reached:

by phone at (760) 728-8787,
or by mail at 2737 Vista del Rio,
Fallbrook, CA 92028.

To order more copies,
call 888-549-0551.

Doug, Mom, and Kelby.

Names indicate people mentioned in the book.

"Money just makes you more of what you are." – Bill Gouldd